# THE STAR WARS ALBUM

The incredible behind-the-scenes story of the most extraordinary motion picture of our time

BALLANTINE BOOKS • NEW YORK

Copyright © 1977 Twentieth Century-Fox Film Corporation. All rights reserved.

All rights reserved under International and Pan-American Copyright Conventions. Published in the United States by Ballantine Books, a division of Random House, Inc., New York, and simultaneously in Canada by Ballantine Books of Canada, Ltd., Toronto, Canada.

Library of Congress Catalog Card Number: 77-93090
ISBN 0-345-27591-8
Manufactured in the United States of America
First Edition: November 1977

## ACKNOWLEDGEMENTS

All of the production photographs from 20th Century-Fox film, *Star Wars,* were taken by Johnny Jay, Gary Kurtz and the photographers at Industrial Light and Magic, Inc. All reproduction shots in the Science Fiction section pages 4-7, were taken by Jurgen Volmer. The editors also gratefully acknowledge the following for their assistance in obtaining information and photographs in this issue: Charles Lippincott, Carol Wikarska, Marc Pevers, Victor Ghidalia, Judy-Lynn del Rey, Tom Bodkin, George Lucas, John Dykstra, Hal Sherman, Supersnipe Comic Art Gallery, Movie Star News and Cinemabilia.

All *Star Wars* photographs and art work © 1977 Twentieth Century-Fox Film Corp. Back cover painting © 1977 Hildebrandt Brothers.

STAR WARS, the biggest motion picture box office hit in history, evolved from George Lucas' life long passion for science fantasy and romantic adventure.

Heroes like Flash Gordon, Tarzan and Errol Flynn were his Saturday afternoon movie house companions.

Films weren't his only inspiration. Tracing back to the beginnings of science fiction, piece by piece, Lucas took the best themes each era of sf literature had to offer and meshed them, creating an unrivaled space fantasy.

We now start our journey where Lucas did — at the beginning.

# How It All Began: Fact or Fiction?

Before there ever was a *Star Wars*, a *2001*, a *Flash Gordon* — or even the phrase "science fiction" — there was the written word.

Through the words of writers like Jules Verne, H.G. Wells, and Edgar Allen Poe, the path to current science fiction was paved.

In looking back over the past eras of sf, a revelation of how prophetic these writers were becomes apparent, when one realizes that their fantasies have now become our reality.

As early as 1863 Jules Verne was writing about the wonders to come from the laboratories of science and engineering. Much later in 1911, Hugo Gernsbeck, the modern day "father of sf," spoke of space travel, fluorescent lighting and jukeboxes in his classic novel, *Ralph 124C41+*. Upon closer inspection of the title, "one to foresee for one" the pun is made evident.

Arthur C. Clark *(2001)* once said, "Good science fiction is the only genuine consciousness expanding drug there is." Tracing back the roots of this "drug," many experts agree that the birth of the science fiction novel started with Cyrano de Bergerac.

In 1650, de Bergerac wrote *A Voyage to the Moon,* in which he sent a group of characters to the moon by rocket ship. Once there, he had them describe what they saw. His descriptions were proved so accurate that experts are even baffled.

Edgar Allen Poe was another major figure in this field. Poe's *Descent into Maelstrom* is considered a major advance because it stressed that every departure from the norm must be logically explained scientifically.

Of all the writers in this form, Jules Verne was one of the most prolific. The root of Verne's world-wide success was in his ability to make technological achievements a subject for fiction. The best known of his works, *Twenty Thousand Leagues Under the Sea,* merges the best of Verne's ideas and characters.

The last of the British imports, H.G. Wells demonstrated that sf was indeed literature. Responsible for some of the most spectacular works: *The Time Machine, The Invisible Man,* to mention only a few, have made Wells one of the most highly respected writers of his time.

Moving up the time-scale and over the Atlantic Ocean — America was also making its mark in the sf genre.

A young man from Luxembourg emigrated to this country in 1904. In 1927 *Amazing Stories,* the most successful "pulp" of all times, was founded and Hugo Gernsbeck, its founder and publisher, had now made his mark.

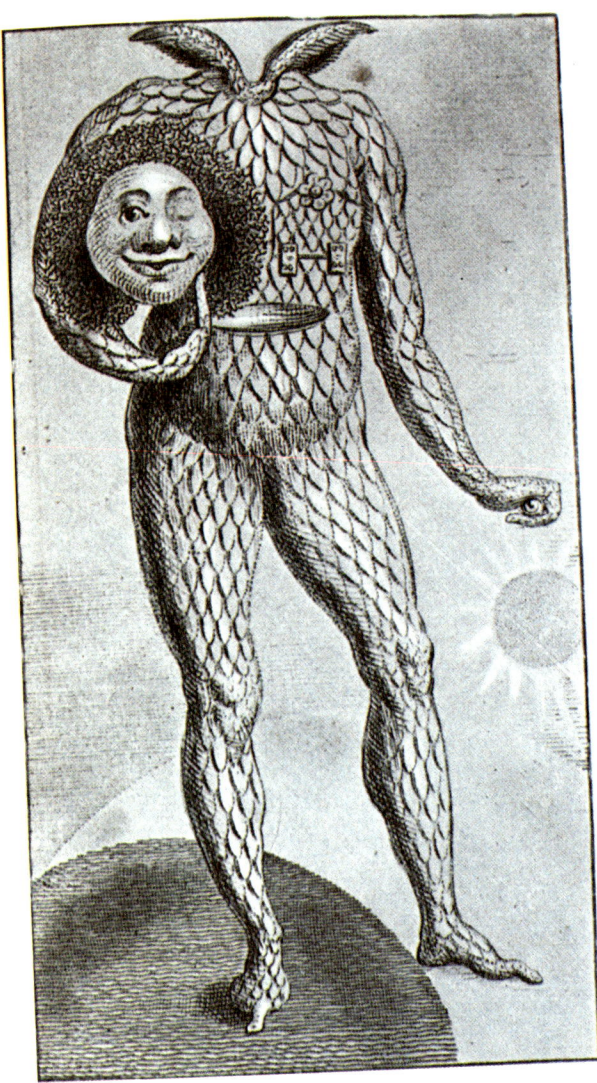

This 1869 illustration by Cruikshank features *The Adventures of Baron Munchausen*. The writer of the series is unknown, but Cruikshank etched each illustration personally. This entry is entitled, *An Inhabitant of the Moon*.

Hugo Gernsbeck stressed literary quality in his magazines ranging from *Popular Science* to pulps like *Amazing Stories*. One of Gernsbeck's inspirational ideas was having literary contests. The winner would have his work published and receive a bold credit on the cover.

*Amazing Stories* was the quantum leap for some of the greatest American science fiction writers. Names like Ray Bradbury, H.G. Wells, and Edgar Rice Burroughs all got their starts and exposure due to Gernsbeck.

5

Original prints of *Flash Gordon* comic strips (top) cost up to two hundred dollars today, as compared to a nickel in 1930. This lobby card (middle), featuring Charles Middleton as Emperor Ming, proved quite a lure to kiddie matinee goers in 1939. Peter Cushing (bottom) as Grand Moff Tarkin bears a striking resemblance to Middleton as Emperor Ming. Could it be that George Lucas cast Cushing because of the similarities?

# Flash: Universal Hero!

As far back as 1911, the movie serial was a basic in the diet of American filmgoers. The most popular star of these was undoubtedly Tom Mix, who, according to trivia buffs, was shot some two hundred times throughout his film career yet never carried a gram of buckshot anywhere on his person in one given installment.

In the early 1930's, a young artist named Alex Raymond introduced Flash Gordon to the funny pages to overwhelming response. It wasn't until 1936, however, that Flash Gordon truly came to life, courtesy of Universal Pictures. Universal's claim to fame at this time was Deanna Durbin, not to mention a steady supply of horror films.

Buster Crabbe was cast as Flash Gordon, Jean Rogers as Dale Arden, the woman in Flash's life, Frank Shannon as Dr. Zarkov and Charles Middleton as the truly nasty Emperor Ming, who was to prove more than a slimy villain for the next five years of Flash Gordon films.

Each episode ran an average of thirty minutes, and there were twelve to fifteen episodes altogether. A new episode was played each week, usually paired with a double feature, a newsreel and several cartoons. From Sunday until the following Saturday, children of the United States lived in perpetual suspense wondering how Flash would manage to save his skin from week to week. Each episode ended with Flash's life in grave danger, whether he was falling in a wind tunnel, wrestling a lion or caught in some other seemingly unescapable situation. He always managed to save himself just in time, however, only to find himself in more trouble at the end.

*Star Wars* writer-director George Lucas was heavily influenced by both Flash Gordon and Buck Rogers. *Buck Rogers* was yet another serial inspired by the success of *Flash Gordon*. Again it featured Buster Crabbe, taking a one year hiatus from his *Flash Gordon* duties.

*Flash Gordon* inspired countless imitations both in movies and later across the television screen. Most of them were fabricated imitations, but some, such as *Superman* for example, went on to achieve cult status of their own. The thirty-minute serializations seemed perfect for a half hour television show.

Originally, Lucas attempted to secure the *Flash Gordon* rights in order to make his own saga. The owners of the rights, however, wanted more than Lucas could pay, prompting him to invent his own character. By viewing the old *Flash Gordon*, it is fairly easy to see where Lucas got much of his inspiration. Indeed, Luke Skywalker bears more than a close resemblance to Flash Gordon.

Both *Flash Gordon* and *Star Wars* lean more heavily on fantasy than on science fiction. *Flash Gordon* is still popular today, and usually turns up on many local television stations across the U.S. and Europe. In an age where films tend toward fear and nightmares, it is certain that *Flash Gordon* and *Star Wars* are healthy diversions.

(Left) This lobby card for Flash Gordon faintly resembles the poster for *Star Wars*.
(Right) Luke Skywalker, a counterpart of Flash, takes steady aim at a stormtrooper.

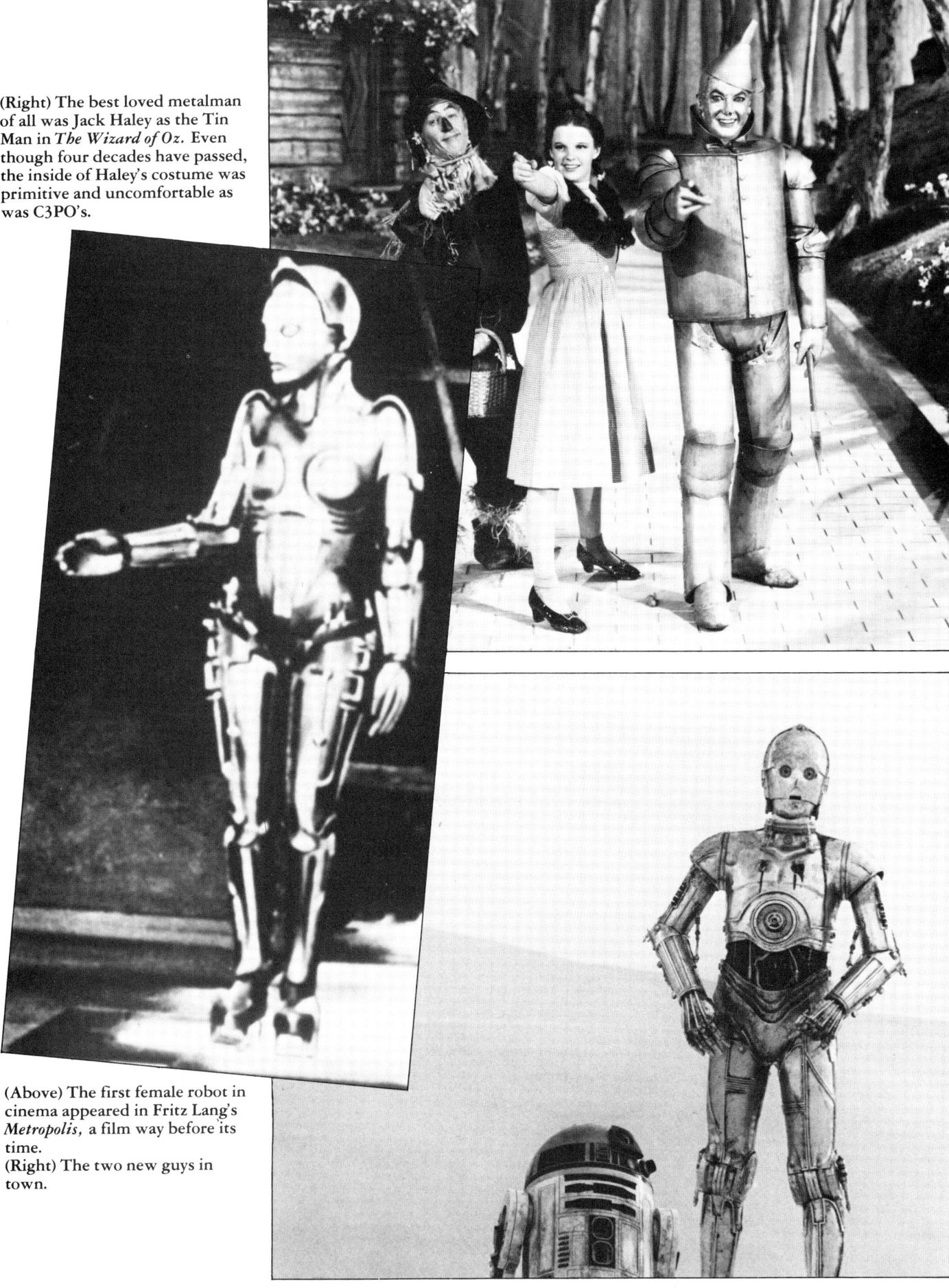

(Right) The best loved metalman of all was Jack Haley as the Tin Man in *The Wizard of Oz*. Even though four decades have passed, the inside of Haley's costume was primitive and uncomfortable as was C3PO's.

(Above) The first female robot in cinema appeared in Fritz Lang's *Metropolis,* a film way before its time.
(Right) The two new guys in town.

# Robot Revolution: Early Relatives of *Star Wars*

While George Lucas created filmdom's first android comedy team, See Threepio and Artoo Detoo, the role of the robot in motion pictures was born long before Mr. Lucas was. Of the two robots, See Threepio proves that it's hard to keep a good robot down. His predecessors speak, gurgle, and chirp for themselves.

The concept of the robot was used to good advantage in *Forbidden Planet,* which introduced a loveable robot named Robby, who cooked and cleaned. Robby's popularity was so great that another film was crafted exclusively for him, a dismal effort called *The Invisible Boy.*

Robert Wise's *The Day the Earth Stood Still,* made in 1951, featured an eight-foot tall and very ominous robot named Gort, who took orders from Klaatu, played by Michael Rennie. Among Gort's functions was restoring Klaatu to life after being shot by a hostile marine. Gort, unlike Threepio, showed no emotion and was programmed only to respond to his master's command.

(Above) In 1956, *Forbidden Planet* gave viewers Robby the Robot. Robby cooked, cleaned and was able to render weapons inoperable.
(Left) *The Day the Earth Stood Still* gave us another indestructible robot, Gort.

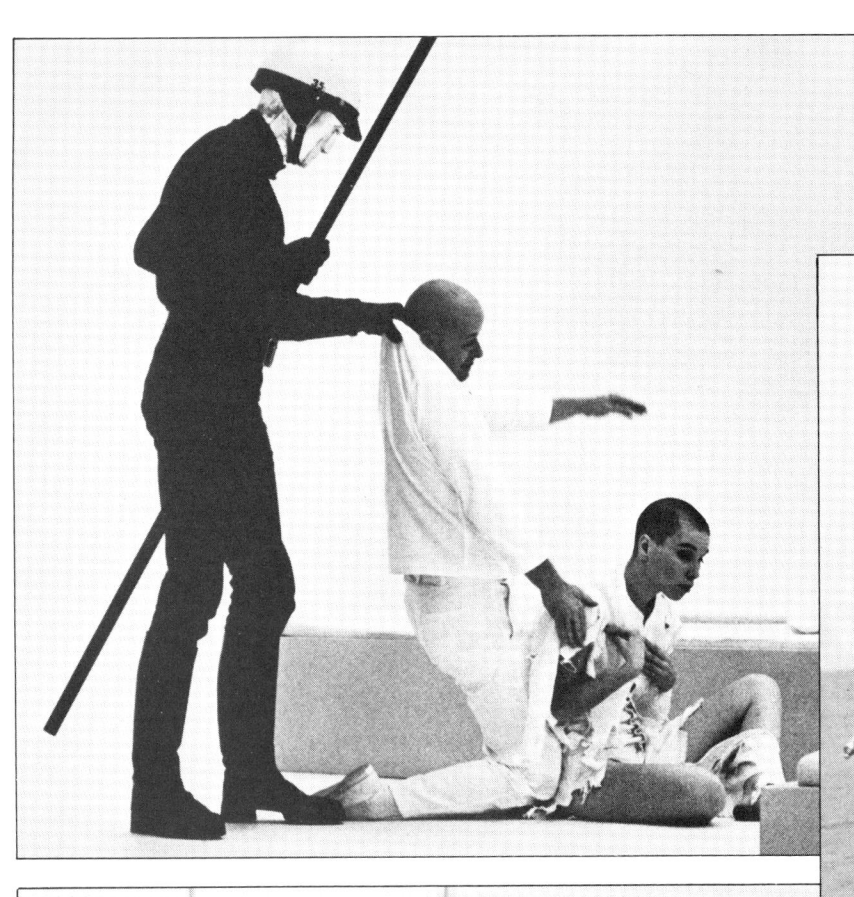

(Left) In George Lucas' first feature, *THX 1138,* he created an underground city where emotion was outlawed; therefore robot police maintained order.

(Above) C3P0 is a composite of many robots throughout film history. What makes him unique are his brisk butler-like mannerisms. (Left) Woody Allen took a detour on the road to futuristics by creating robots in *Sleeper* who were butlers that ran amok.

For the most part, the robot in science fiction, is usually cold and calculating, as in Fritz Lang's *Metropolis*. In Woody Allen's *Sleeper* however, the robot was turned to a comic asset, with Allen romping around in whiteface, impersonating a robot strikingly similar to See Threepio.

Jack Haley Sr.'s Tin Man in the *Wizard of Oz* was highly reminiscent of a robot. Indeed, he walked like one and was designed like one; he was the most human of all. Most recently, though, Threepio's closest relative appeared in *Logan's Run*.

(Above) In *Logan's Run,* robots and computers controlled the environment that Michael York lived in.
(Upper right) R2D2 is one of a kind when it comes to robotics, but his closest relative probably came out of *Freaks*.
(Lower Right) Todd Browning's *Freaks* made in 1931 and banned for thirty years in the U.S. The legless wonder, pictured here, was an early predecessor of Artoo Detoo.

# The Monstrous Misfits

In creating *Star Wars*, director Lucas apparently allowed his creative mind to run amok. Not content to revive a seriously flagging genre, he also bolstered *Star Wars'* appeal by sprinkling other favorite film genres into his intergalactic Mulligan's Stew.

The cantina scene in *Star Wars*, aside from jolting the already hyperactive audience, incorporated goons from the best horror movies Hollywood produced in its heyday. In viewing the bizarre and surreal scene, one feels a bit of deja vu, almost as if he'd seen the creation in another movie.

Tod Browning's *Freaks* is the most notable here. Made in 1931 and banned in the U.S. for some thirty years afterward, *Freaks* still carries the ability to shock viewers, with the same impact it had when first released. One is reminded of *Freaks* while watching the cantina scene, just as he is reminded of the 1955 epic *This Island Earth*, which featured two mutant spacemen that strongly resembled the web fingered musicians in the cantina bar scene. Visually stunning, *This Island Earth* remains one of the finest features Hollywood has ever produced.

Boris Karloff's Frankenstein, Charles Laughton's *The Hunchback of Notre Dame* and Lon Chaney's Wolfman all played a part in *Star Wars'* cantina sequence. Chewbacca, the Wookiee, almost seems a direct decendent of Lawrence Talbot, the unfortunate Wolfman. The Banthas, those hideous animals, appeared in a slightly altered form in Walt Disney's *Fantasia*.

(Top) Boris Karloff as Frankenstein, circa 1931. The passing years have not lessened the film's shock impact.
(Middle) Lon Chaney Jr. stands ready to bite some unsuspecting victim as the Wolfman. The resemblence to a Wookiee is obvious.
(Right) Not one of the cantina muscians, but rather a creature from *This Island Earth*, an sf classic.

(Right) Universal's *The Creature From the Black Lagoon*, who sent more children to bed with nightmares than any other monster of the fifties.

(Above) This charming fellow appeared on a segment of *The Outer Limits*, a popular television show of the Sixties, but could easily be confused with one of the cantina residents.
(Right) John Wayne and Montgomery Clift in *The Searchers*, a classic western shoot-em-up that inspired George Lucas while he was creating the cantina scene.

## Teammates in Comedy

Perhaps the world's best known and best loved comedy team was the ingenious union of skinny Stan Laurel and fat Oliver Norvell Hardy. What distinguished Laurel and Hardy from other comedy teams was the rapport that existed between the two. In their films, Stan and Ollie were totally devoted to each other, even when they were shown as married men.

The Thirties represented an era of film comedy that cannot be recaptured, so one may think. But George Lucas sees otherwise, having created a comedy team that will be remembered long after the profits to *Star Wars* have been reinvested, namely, See Threepio and Artoo Detoo. What makes these two inorganic funnymen different from any other comedy team is that they are androids. Artoo Detoo, short and squat, and See Threepio, tall and lanky, find themselves in situations comparable to those that Laurel and Hardy often found themselves up against.

Both Artoo and Threepio were as real to director Lucas as they were to anyone who has seen the film and loved the pranks the two droids pulled off.

The man behind Threepio—literally was actor Anthony Daniels, while Kenny Baker was only a part-time Artoo Detoo, having had two twin brothers throughout the filming.

The mannerisms of Stan Laurel and Oliver Hardy have been emulated through the years by many, but it took two droids to really do it right.

"Tarzan" figures prominently here. In the character of Luke Skywalker, director Lucas has instilled a brand of courage that has been on vacation since the last Tarzan movie. Johnny Weissmuller's Tarzan was fearless, and for someone who had no education, he always managed somehow to rescue Jane or his son, Boy. Be it ten thousand rampaging pygmies of Imperial stormtroopers, the hero will always find his way clear of a sticky situation.

While Mark Hamill may lack a brawny chest or the ability to yodel like Tarzan, he still represents a singular kind of hero that audiences can relate to.

Luke and Leia do their part as swingers in the grand old tradition of Tarzan and Jane, who were responsible for making swinging a popular pastime. Johnny Weissmuller and Maureen O'Sullivan starred in a series of *Tarzan* films during the Thirties. They are shown regularly on television all over the world. What's more, *Tarzan* went on to outgrow Weissmuller and went through a succession of he-men who portrayed the Edgar Rice Burroughs hero in both film and television.

## On Guard!

Lucas doesn't stop there though, going on to puncture a hole or two in the swashbuckler, another era that hasn't seen the darkness of a movie house in quite some time. To see Darth Vader and Ben Kenobi finally come face to face in the long anticipated duel brings back images of Burt Lancaster romping in *The Crimson Pirate,* or Errol Flynn in *Captain Blood.* Still playing on late shows all over the country, these old movies prove that they don't make films like they used to.

It was, and still is, the stuff dreams are made of. In trying to revive an era and style of filmmaking that has seemingly given way to colder, brasher films, Lucas meshes these genres like a piece of well oiled machinery. The majority of film-goers will be unaware of Lucas' technique unless they are avid film buffs. For the young and old alike, Ben and Darth will achieve the same immortality in *Star Wars* as Basil Rathbone and Tyrone Power have in the *Mark of Zorro.*

(Top) Ben Kenobi and Darth Vader cross lightsabers, á la *Scaramouche.*
(Bottom) Errol Flynn grins devilishly, pointing his sword at an unseen enemy in *Captain Blood.*

(Top right) Tyrone Power and Basil Rathbone both mean business in *The Mark of Zorro*.
(Middle) In a scene from *Knights of the Round Table*, these two knights prove that chivalry is quite dead.
(Bottom) Stewart Granger bests his rival in a scene from *Scaramouche*.

# "Get Out of Town Before the Twin Suns Set."

One almost wishes at various intervals that one of the pug uglies in the cantina would utter a line like "this planet ain't big enough for the both of us," or "Imperial Raider speak with forked tongue."

Han Solo's little speech "I been from one end of this galaxy to the other. I seen a lotta strange things," derives basically from movies like *The Searchers,* a western, or a completely different genre, from a film such as *Bwana Devil.* Han Solo recreates the macho, loner image, the kind that made actors like Kirk Douglas, Robert Mitchum, Richard Widmark and others rise to fame. Lean, wiry and ever-cautious, Han Solo more or less stumbles through one pitfall after another.

It has been the goal of numerous movie makers to attempt to recreate the atmosphere and style of vintage dramas, comedies and other kinds of movies which haven't been seen since the big studios shut down production with the advent of television.

Should one look hard enough, he will find many similarities to a lot of the old movies shown on late night television. Lucas has taken great pains to inject old-time movie magic back into *Star Wars*.

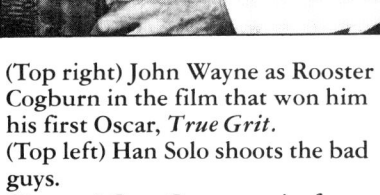

(Top right) John Wayne as Rooster Cogburn in the film that won him his first Oscar, *True Grit*.
(Top left) Han Solo shoots the bad guys.
(Bottom) Gary Cooper waits for his own showdown in the 1954 movie, *High Noon*.

(Top) The Shadow makes a rare personal appearance.
(Bottom) An ominous Darth Vader grabs a Rebel.

# The Mystique

Although The Shadow was heard and not seen, his contributions to law and order were priceless. In much the same way Ben Kenobi, the last of the Jedi Knights, used the ways of The Force in the same fashion. Ben points out though that where there is good, there is evil. Darth Vader is the prime example, being seduced by the dark side of The Force. On a similar plane as The Force, The Shadow had the effect to mesmerize the weak-minded into doing anything he wanted, as Ben Kenobi did to the Imperial Soldiers.

An Imperial Cruiser in hot pursuit of Princess Leia's ship. The Imperial ship has little trouble catching the Rebel craft.

# Damsel in Distress

A LONG time ago in a galaxy far, far away...high above the planet of Tatooine, a galactic cruiser is in the midst of a somewhat vain attempt to outrun a massive Imperial cruiser. The Imperial cruiser, with its dozens of heavy weapon implacements jutting out of it like some metal cactus, is determined to capture its prey. There is no way out for the galactic cruiser, those aboard know their efforts of escape are useless.

As explosions and high powered laser rays riddle the body of the galactic cruiser, See Threepio, a tall golden man-like machine and Artoo Detoo, a stubby, tripodal robot, are scurrying about.

"Did you hear that?" Threepio inquires in his indignant British voice, "They've shut down the main reactor and the drive...madness, sheer madness, this time we'll be destroyed for sure." Artoo doesn't seem to be too affected by Threepio's hysterics...a safe corner is all he wants.

Suddenly, the chaos comes to a halt as the Imperial cruiser hovers over the powerless galactic ship and scoops it up through gravitational pull.

For a moment, there is complete silence.

The shriek of overstressed metal fills the air as white metal beads begin dropping to the corridor floor. While Threepio and Artoo peer out from behind the shelter of their alcove, they discover their new arrivals are human Imperial stormtroopers in armor, no mechanicals.

Through the pockets of smoke and the lightning bolts, the dark, menacing shape of Lord Darth Vader appears. Clad in a hideous, grilled breathing mask, Vader's stormtroopers pave the way for him. His mission—to get the data that has been intercepted.

Meanwhile, as Threepio scrambles about searching for his friend Artoo, he comes upon a strange sight. Up ahead, a young woman, Princess Leia Organa, a member of the Rebel Alliance, whose goal is to stop the maniacal Darth Vader, starts feeding messages into Artoo. With the stomping sound of stormtroopers--Princess Leia quickly disappears into the interior of the cruiser.

Darth Vader's Storm Troopers taking over Princess Leia's ship, killing all her soldiers.

Princess Leia feeds R2D2 plans. She programs him to escape and deliver the news to Obi-Wan Kenobi.

"Don't play games with me, Your Highness. You aren't on any mercy mission this time."

C3PO and R2D2 jettison out of Princess Leia's captured ship towards Tatooine.

See Threepio and Artoo Detoo part company on the desert wastes of Tatooine.

# Artoo Detoo and See Threepio: Quick Getaway

ARTOO urges his counterpart Threepio to board one of the escape pods. Naturally, Threepio has reservations, as the escape pods are for organics only. Artoo ignores Threepio's incessant, babbling protests and awkwardly slips into it. Threepio, having no other course, reluctantly follows, muttering "I'm going to regret this..."

Like a cork shooting out of a pop gun, the two droids jettison from the Rebel cruiser into space away from the Imperial cruiser. The pod is spotted however, and an officer of the Imperial ship prepares to destroy it. His commanding officer informs him that since there are no life forms aboard, he need not bother.

With most of the Rebel soldiers dead or dying, Princess Leia attempts to flee the Rebel ship. An Imperial stormtrooper zaps her with a ray gun, stunning her momentarily. She is brought to Darth, who questions her about the plans which were beamed aboard the ship. She denies all of course, much to Vader's chagrin.

Vader orders two officers to retrieve the jettisoned pod from Tatooine, knowing the missing plans are somewhere aboard.

One of Vader's assistants, however, seems less assured as to the sanity of Vader's plan. He fears that Vader's plan will cause the Senate to side with the Rebel Alliance.

Vader instructs him to send a transmission, saying all on board were killed. Vader establishes himself as a true meanie, who will stop at nothing to destroy the last remnants of the Rebel Alliance. His assistant assures the dark Lord Vader that Princess Leia will not betray the Rebellion.

"Leave that to me," Vader replies.

The Jawas, a race of scavengers on Tatooine, carry an immobilized Artoo Detoo off to their immense Sandcrawler.

# Will R2D2 C3PO Again?

ARTOO and Threepio land smack in the middle of miles of wasteland known as the Tatooine Deserts. At once the pair starts bickering about which way to go. As might be expected, Threepio sets off in one direction, convinced that Artoo's fate is doomed, since he went off in the other direction.

After walking miles and seeing nothing except a skeleton of a huge dinosaur, Threepio's future as a droid looks bleak. Then, he spots something moving on the far horizon. Threepio pleads for help, unaware of what fate awaits him.

Meanwhile, Artoo scoots through rocky terrain. The twin suns of Tatooine gradually vanish and his surroundings become dark and mysterious. His android's sense of danger is aroused; he knows there are creatures somewhere about. His hunches prove accurate.

The Jawas, little rodent like beings, zap Artoo with their weapons, immobilizing him instantly. Deactivated, he is transported to an enormous Sandcrawler.

The insides of the Sandcrawler resemble a droid warehouse. Hundreds of misshapen robots, all sizes, shapes, and functions, wait to be sold or melted down. Artoo meets none other than Threepio, victim of a similar fate. The two are ecstatic about their reunion, though their ultimate fate seems unknown.

Artoo is sucked up into the depths of the Sandcrawler.

With stormtroopers everywhere, things begin to look gloomy.

Darth Vader's dirtymen land on Tatooine.

A stormtrooper riding a prehistoric resident of Tatooine.

# "Get Me Those Tapes"

DARTH Vader, not sure the jettisoned pod was just a malfunction decides to send down his Imperial soldiers to retrieve it. "If those data tapes were in the pod they must be retrieved at any cost," says Vader.

"As you wish," the commander acknowledges.

The Soldiers land on Tatooine and find the empty pod. "Nothing," the inspecting trooper mutters to several of his companions. "No tapes, and no sign of habitation, yet it set down intact."

"Droids, it's the only answer," another officer says.

They must follow the tracks and locate Artoo Detoo and See Threepio before the tapes get into the wrong hands. The survival of the Death Star depends on it.

C3P0 forlorn and lost in the sands of Tatooine meets up with the remains of another victim. Seeing what looks like help up ahead, he tries waving them down. His rescue team turns out to be the Jawas' Sandcrawler. They zap C3P0 and fling him in with the rest of the scrap metal they've found.

Once inside the Sandcrawl which resembles a futuris junk yard, he is reunit with his squat counterpa R2D2 in the most touchi scene in the film. So their excitement we off when they realize th the worst is yet to con Will they be melted? will they simply be sold another master?

As Luke inspects the droids—C3PO is joyous to find that he and R2D2 will remain a team.

# "This Is Another Fine Mess You've Gotten Me Into"

BACK on Tatooine, the Jawas unload their menagerie of droids and put them up for sale. Two prospective buyers, Owen Lars and his nephew, twenty-year-old Luke Skywalker, begin to survey the collection. Proceeding to the end of the line, Owen, a farmer by trade, begins to peer at the sand-scoured but still flashy bronze finish of the tall humanoid.

"I need," Owen began, "a droid that knows the binary language of moisture vaporators."

"Vaporators!" Threepio exclaims, "We are both in luck sir, my first job was programming binary load lifters, very similar to your vaporators in most respects."

Still hesitant, Owen finally agrees to take Threepio. Moving further down the line, the farmer decides to buy one more droid, this time an Artoo unit—but not Artoo Detoo.

As the Jawas begin ushering the unsold goods back into their Sandcrawler, Luke glances back to discover that the Artoo unit they've taken has petered out. This infuriates his uncle who accuses the sneaky Jawas of peddling shoddy merchandise.

In order to appease him, the Jawas agree to a trade. Threepio jumps at the chance of putting in a word for his buddy, Artoo Detoo. "Excuse me, sir, but that R-2 unit is in prime condition. A real bargain. I don't believe these creatures have any idea what good shape he's really in. Don't let all the sand and dust deceive you."

Luke's uncle, already irritated by the whole incident, agrees to trade for Artoo Detoo.

Although Threepio is ecstatic about being reunited with his sidekick, Artoo, he puts on a very indifferent air.

C3PO relaxes in his oil bath hoping his perilous journey has ended.

# Runaway Robot

AT Uncle Owen's request, Luke starts cleaning out the new androids. Threepio tells Luke about the war between the Imperials and Rebels, but can only offer sketchy details.

As Luke is cleaning the carbon from Artoo's innards, part of Princess Leia's message is beamed. As he sees her animated form, Luke is instantly captivated by her beauty.

"Obi-Wan Kenobi," the Princess pleads, "help me. You're my only hope."

Luke grills Artoo, but the little android refuses to relay the remainder of the message, insisting it's old data and apparently useless.

At dinner with his Aunt Beru and Uncle Owen, Luke informs his uncle that he wants to leave and enter the Space Academy along with his friends. Uncle Owen refuses him because he needs Luke's help on the moisture farm. Dismayed, Luke sets about his task of getting the androids ready for service on the farm.

Luke leaves the dinner table to go back to the workshop. He finds Threepio hiding behind a wall. Threepio immediately starts babbling about his android counterpart, claiming Artoo left to seek Obi-Wan Kenobi.

Luke is furious as is Threepio, who also worries for his friend's safety. Visions of Sandpeople, needless to say, is not far from Luke's mind.

Instead of going after Artoo that same night, he has to wait until the following morning. The Sandpeople are out and about. Tatooine's desert waste lands prove dangerous after the planet's twin suns set.

Scanning the surrounding countryside with his macrobinoculars, Luke is able to see for miles. Artoo is nowhere to be seen. Luke also feels to blame, having removed Artoo's restraining bolt in order to see the play-out of Princess Leia's message. "That little droid's going to get me into a lot of trouble," Luke groans. Threepio immediately replies, "Oh, he excels at that, Sir."

Luke discusses his future with his aunt and uncle. When he asks about going to the Academy, his uncle denies him permission and tells him his help is still needed on the farm.

Perched on his Bantha, a Tusken Raider surveys the area.

Luke scans the scene for trouble.

# Watch Out, Sandpeople!

THE following morning, Luke and Threepio set off in his landspeeder, a jet propelled car. They meet up with Artoo, who babbles about his mission to find Obi-Wan Kenobi. He also detects another presence—Sandpeople. Threepio wants to flee, but Luke wants to take a closer look.

Sure enough, he sees several Banthas—ugly beasts that look like a cross between a rhino and a dinosaur. Scanning the site again, Luke is attacked and knocked unconscious by one of the Sandpeople. Terrified, Threepio falls over and disappears from view.

Suddenly, a low bellowing cry is heard from the surrounding mountains and the Sandpeople flee, leaving Luke's motionless body lying near the landspeeder. A dark, shrouded figure approaches. It is Ben Kenobi.

He revives Luke, who is well aware of Ben's awesome reputation. "The Sandpeople are easily frightened," Ben Kenobi informs them, "but they'll be back and in greater numbers."

A Tusken Raider darts out and attacks Luke.

# Obi-Wan Kenobi Comes out of Retirement

THE slightly dismantled Threepio, Luke, and Artoo return to Ben's sparse cave. Once there, Luke begins the arduous task of re-attaching Threepio's arm to the rest of him.

With Luke busy, Ben begins fiddling with Artoo in search of the message he's supposedly carrying.

An instant later the striking portrait of Princess Leia is projected into the empty space from the front of the little robot.

"Yes, I think I've got it," Kenobi murmurs. The image once again begins to flicker.

She said, "Information vital to the survival of the Alliance has been secured in the mind of this Detoo droid. My father will know how to retrieve it. I plead with you to see this unit safely delivered to Alderaan."

Ben plays the message over several times. After Luke completes his work, Ben presents Luke with his father's lightsaber. Luke then learns that both Ben and his father served as Jedi Knights and fought in the Clone Wars together.

After darting the light saber around for a few minutes, Luke then asks Ben how his father lost his life. Ben explains that his father was betrayed by another young Jedi Knight, Darth Vader, who later murdered him.

Several minutes pass and Ben finally asks Luke to join him in Alderaan. Luke then explains he is committed to helping his uncle on their farm.

On his way back home, Luke discovers the Jawas' Sandcrawler is decimated. Realizing only Imperial forces would mount an attack with that kind of cold accuracy, Luke races back, only to find the inevitable.

There lying in the billowing smoke are the remains of Owen and his wife Beru.

Ben and Luke talk about The Force while fixing up C3PO. Princess Leia's message is soon to be discovered.

The four make their entry into Mos Eisley, Ben uses The Force to prevent stormtroopers from asking questions.

The task that awaits Ben Kenobi and Luke is to get Artoo to Alderaan so that the plans to the Death Star can be retrieved by the Rebels.

The four journey to Mos Eisley, a spaceport and clearinghouse for Tatooine's low-life. Knowing the best pilots are at the cantina, Ben searches out Han Solo, who may be willing to take them to Alderaan.

Unaware they're being trailed, the group attempts to flee Mos Eisley. Their efforts are sidetracked as Imperial Troopers try to foil the escape. Solo, whose prowess matches his bragging, lifts off and makes it into space, beating out an Imperial Cruiser.

Aboard the Death Star, Tarkin orders the peaceful planet of Alderaan to be destroyed.

Suddenly Solo informs them that Alderaan is nothing more than a mass of cinders. To make matters worse, Solo finds himself face to face with the ominous Death Star. The powerful tracking beam being projected from the Death Star proves too strong for the Falcon to buck, and they are pulled into its reaches.

The five travelers seek refuge in the cargo area of the ship which is usually reserved for Solo's smuggling ventures. As the Imperial soldiers make a routine inspection of the craft, they are zapped dead, and their uniforms are taken by Luke and Solo. Together, the five steal their way into a control room where they seize power by killing the technicians. Ben leaves the others to accomplish his own dual mission: he must shut down the trackbeam so the Rebels may escape; and he must find his former protegé—now gone bad—Darth Vader.

After Luke discovers the Jawas' Sandcrawler decimated, he returns to his farm only to find the burned remains of his aunt and uncle.

35

Luke, Ben, Han Solo and Chewbacca discuss their plans to leave Mos Eisley and head towards Alderaan.

Han Solo and Chewbacco blowing up the controls to release Princess Leia from her cell.

The brave foursome trapped in the garbage dump. Their only hope is to contact the droids who can prevent the walls from caving in.

# The Good Guys Meet the Bad Guys

ARTOO hooks his arm into a socket and discovers that the Princess is somewhere aboard the Death Star. Scanning a readout of the ship, Luke and Solo find that she's in one of the detention cells. With Chewbacca handcuffed to look like a prisoner, they make their way to the detention block. Luke releases the Princess and all four find themselves sealed off from every escape route. With no other way out, the four of them dive through a hole the Princess blasts with Luke's gun. They land in the garbage chamber, up to their ears in muck. To make matters worse, a snake-like creature swims through the murky garbage and wraps itself around Luke's ankle, dragging him down into the black liquid.

The situation looks bleakest when the walls of the garbage hatch begin to close in around them, making the chamber smaller and smaller. Solo quips, "We're all gonna be a lot thinner."

Frantically, Luke cries into his radio unit ordering Artoo to shut down the controls before it's too late. He and Threepio are hiding out near the heavily guarded Falcon when Luke's plea comes through. Acting quickly, Artoo deactivates the controls and shuts down the garbage mashers, just in time.

Meanwhile, Ben is busy elsewhere. Like a ghost in the night, he steals through the Death Star and manages to shut down the tractor beam, a gravitational ray that acts as a force field, and draws anything that comes close into the clutches of the Death Star.

On their way back to the Falcon, Luke, Leia, Solo and Chewy run smack into a group of Imperial stormtroopers.

Solo heads off the Imperial soldiers while Luke and the Princess flee in the opposite direction. They find themselves trapped once more. The door is sealed off behind them, with nothing but a bottomless shaftway in front of them. There doesn't appear to be any way out. Luke, in a rush of quick thinking, produces a long, thin, wire-like stringing apparatus and uses it to swing himself and the Princess from one end of the shaftway to the other side.

Artoo Detoo and Threepio frantically attempt to shut down the garbage mashers before Luke and the others get compacted.

Luke and Leia, à la Tarzan and Jane, make a death defying leap across the black abyss of the Death Star.

Ben and Darth finally meet. One of them will certainly die, but who will really win in the end?

# Ben and Darth Duel to the Death

BEN and his one time pupil Darth Vader finally meet. Both know that one of them will meet death in a battle to the finish. Ben warns Vader, "Dead, I'll be even more powerful than you can possibly imagine."

After a long series of exhaustive chases, the foursome meet up, and along with their devoted androids, make their way back to the Falcon.

Ben sees that the mission is all but accomplished. He bows to Darth, who delivers the final blow and leaves him for dead. But Ben's threat still lives.

Luke cries out upon seeing Ben die, and attracts the attention of the Imperial soldiers who immediately open fire. Nonetheless, they make their escape from the Death Star, thanks to Ben, who turned off the tractorbeam.

Solo is ecstatic, what with the skillful escape and the prospect of a reward before him for rescuing Princess Leia. She on the other hand, is not so sure. "We're being tracked," she informs the cocky Han. "It's the only explanation for the ease of our escape."

The tired Rebels finally make their way back to the Rebel base on the planet of Yavin, unaware that they are indeed being tracked by the Death Star, which plans to destroy Yavin and the remaining Alliance.

It is soon realized there is only one way for the Death Star to be destroyed: a shot must be fired into a small thermo exhaust chamber, a series of mechanisms will then trigger themselves, ultimately detonating the Death Star. It's a longshot, but The Force is with him, and Luke is certain he can accomplish what seems impossible.

Boarding their Incom T-65 fighters, the few Rebel pilots head for the Death Star, which is quickly approaching Yavin. Luke tries to persuade Solo to join the Rebels, but to Solo the mercenary, Luke's idea of bravery is sheer suicide.

Luke and the others, guided by The Force, veer their way to the fast-approaching Death Star. T.I.E. fighters manage to knock out most of the under-equipped Rebel pilots. A scant Rebel crew remains when Darth Vader decides to get in on the action!

(Top) The hair-raising climax comes to a dizzying finale.
(Middle) Princess Leia, C3PO, and an advisor watch the battle unfold and wait to find out about the future of the Rebel Alliance.

(Left) Luke and Han retur[n] home jubilant after their victor[y]. The Death Star has been destro[y]ed and the Rebel Alliance can no[w] go on living in peace with the re[st] of the galaxy.

# The Reward: Now Who Gets the Princess?

DARTH Vader has managed to shoot down all the Rebel fighters, except Luke. Vader is moving in fast. It looks like certain death for Luke, that is, until Han Solo comes to the rescue and sends Darth Vader plummeting through space.

Using his powers, Luke is able to take the necessary shots at the Death Star and destroy it within seconds of the countdown that will destroy the Rebel base on Yavin.

Luke, Han and Chewy disembark from their flyers to a rousing welcome. In her glee, Princess Leia hugs each of the heroes, including Chewy, whom she'd described earlier as "a walking rug."

Artoo is a mess. Threepio offers his circuits in the hopes that they will help his android chum.

See Threepio and Artoo Detoo, cleaned and polished, stand on the side lines and watch the heroes being presented with spectacular medals from Princess Leia. She offers a smile of thanks to each of them. The galaxy is free once again.

R2D2 and C3PO are spruced up for the ceremony.

Han Solo, Luke and Chewbacca receive their medals for saving the Rebel Alliance.

# The Force Within George Lucas

If one took a jigger of *Stagecoach*, a pinch of *Captain Blood*, a teaspoon of *The Wizard of Oz* and a tat of *The Sands of Iwo Jima*, he just might have *Star Wars*. This is the finest and most spectacular fantasy story ever to hit celluloid. *Star Wars* could possibly be referred to as sort of an intergalactic *Gone With the Wind*, with a planet called Tatooine, light years away from Tara and Rhett Butler.

Never in the history of motion pictures has a film had the impact that *Star Wars* is having, on adults and children alike. In what looked like another dry summer of typical movie fare, *Star Wars* was as welcome as a sun shower, as was demonstrated by the fifty-four million dollars grossed at box-offices all over the country. This is only the beginning; *Star Wars,* within a month of its release became one of the top ten all time box office champs. At this writing, it's edging out *Jaws* for the numero uno spot.

When Alec Guinness read the original script, he refused the part of Ben Kenobi. It wasn't his style. Wanting Guinness to play Ben, Lucas rewrote the part. Making *Star Wars* for Lucas was an excruciatingly painful experience. He considers himself a film maker, not a director. Lucas ultimately likes to sit down behind a camera, shoot and then cut and watch the magic come together.

44

George Lucas and his crew get an overview of the Tunisian desert before setting up for the next shot.

To director George Lucas, *Star Wars* was more than a pet project. Rather, Lucas saw it as a return to fantasy Saturday morning kiddie matinees like Buck Rogers and Flash Gordon. Since then the Western genre seems to have bitten the dust somewhere along the line, as have swash bucklers like *The Crimson Pirate* and *The Swords of Ali Baba,* which had a young Tony Curtis proclaim, "We have come ta' storm da' castle."

"It's a lot of fun," says director Lucas, "that's the word for this movie. Young people today don't have a fantasy life anymore; not the way we did. All the films they see are movies of disasters and realistic violence."

In Lucas' case, he almost met an untimely demise in order to prove his point.

At the age of twenty-five, in 1970, Lucas offered to the public his first full length effort, *THX 1138,* a science fiction saga more in the tradition of *2001.* While the reviews for *THX 1138* were favorable for the most part, the public in general took little notice, because the film fared poorly at the box office.

It wasn't until the summer of 1973 that George Lucas really made his mark. Filmed in less than a month and on a shoestring budget, *American Graffiti* managed to capture the hearts of ninety percent of the under-thirty-

five population, all of whom flocked to see what was essentially a fond biography of Lucas' youth. Nonetheless, the film possessed great charm and an affection for the sixties all or most filmmakers missed.

"I wasted four years of my life cruising around like the kids in *American Graffiti,* Lucas says, "and now I'm on an intergalactic dream of heroism. In *Star Wars,* I'm telling the story of me."

How much of Luke Skywalker is the true George Lucas is anyone's guess, but the more the better. With *Star Wars* Lucas blends the best elements of science fiction, but, unlike many of his peers, doesn't forget the adventure.

(Below) George Lucas talks to Anthony Daniels, See Threepio, about costume problems. Between the weight of his suit, and the heat in the desert, Daniels collapsed many times during the Tunisia shootings.
(Below left) Sandstorms in Tunisia created major difficulties for cast and crew. Everyone except actors had to wear goggles and the camera had to be wrapped in plastic and cleaned thoroughly each night.

(Above) Lucas and Hamill confer about a coming scene.

47

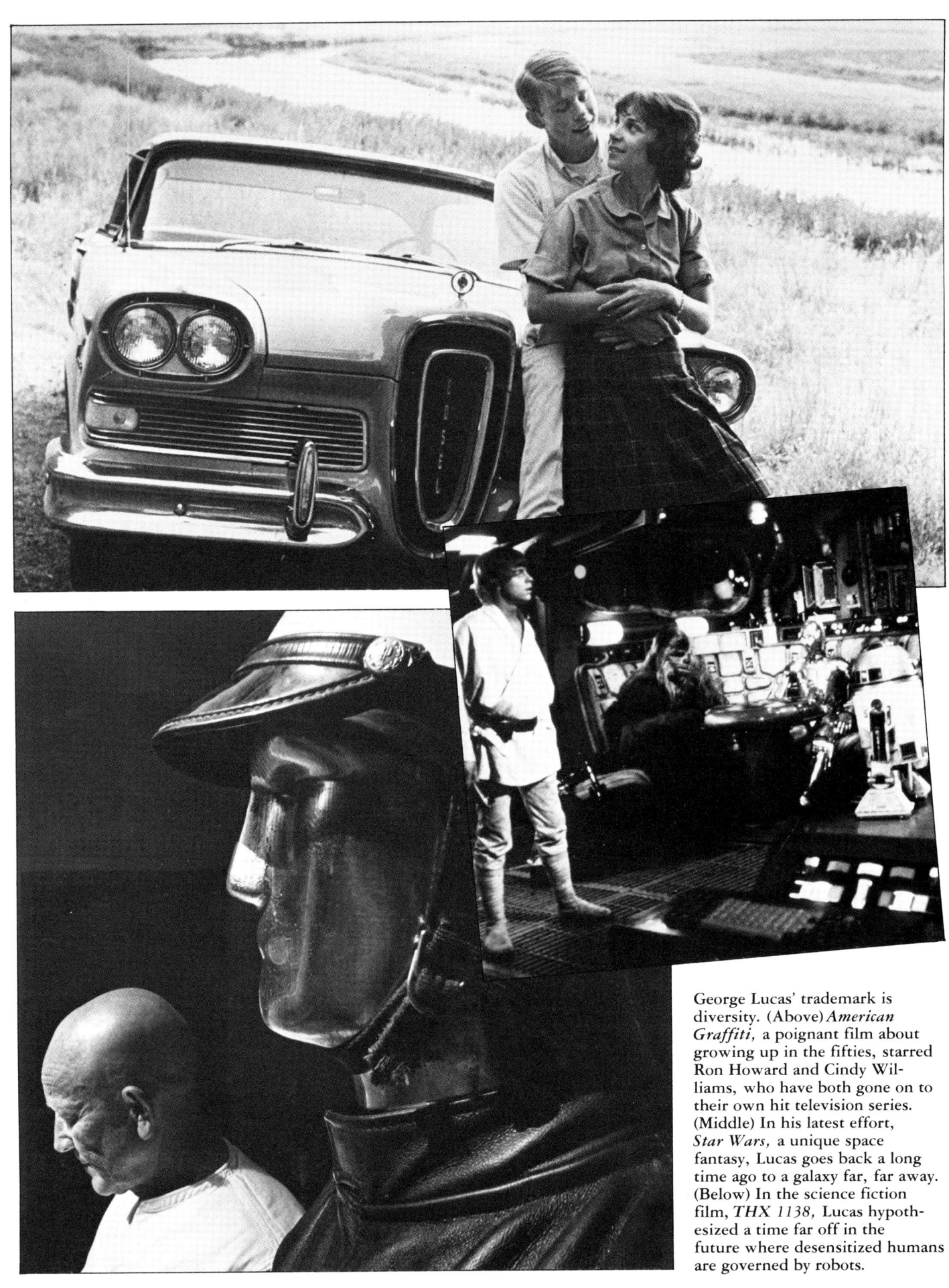

George Lucas' trademark is diversity. (Above) *American Graffiti,* a poignant film about growing up in the fifties, starred Ron Howard and Cindy Williams, who have both gone on to their own hit television series. (Middle) In his latest effort, *Star Wars,* a unique space fantasy, Lucas goes back a long time ago to a galaxy far, far away. (Below) In the science fiction film, *THX 1138,* Lucas hypothesized a time far off in the future where desensitized humans are governed by robots.

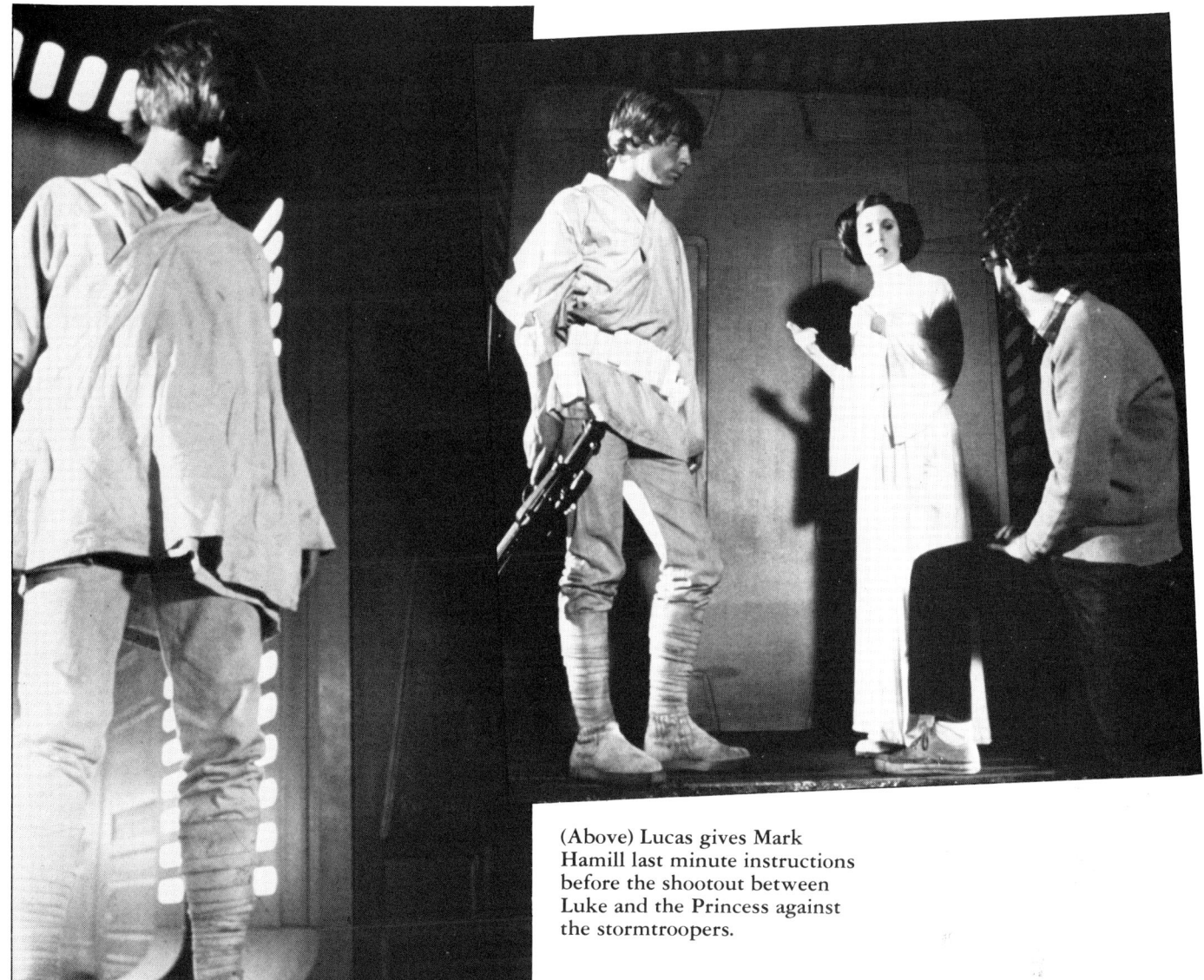

(Above) Lucas gives Mark Hamill last minute instructions before the shootout between Luke and the Princess against the stormtroopers.

"Kids today seem to be having a very boring childhood," Lucas comments, "and I wanted to make something to relieve that boredom. Kids may be a lot more worldly than they were, but I still think they'd like to have some sort of honest, clean...I mean, they should be able to go to the movies and see *something!*

"The reason I made *Star Wars* is that I wanted to give young people some sort of faraway, exotic environment for their imaginations to run free," he adds.

After what had to be one of the most inauspicious beginnings of any film in the history of movies, *Star Wars* proves that hard work and true perseverance do indeed pay off. As long as four years ago, Lucas was tossing around ideas for a space adventure.

Lucas first went to United Artists and proposed the idea of a Flash Gordon-type space saga to the big brass. "It was exciting," he claimed, "a James Bond adventure." United Artists tactfully said no, as did Universal. Both studios, needless to say, are now preparing imitations of the film they themselves turned down.

Twentieth Century-Fox, who gave the world Shirley Temple, *Planet of the Apes* and Mel Brooks to name a few, saw the potential in Lucas' twelve page outline and fronted him the money to finish the script. No slacker, Lucas gave them four scripts all told, all of which ended up as the finished *Star Wars.*

Some of the problems in making *Star Wars* ranged from having to create an original genre in an attempt to explain to a board of directors just *what* a Wookiee was. There were countless flies in the ointment with the robots as well. Artoo Detoo for instance was duplicated some four times before filming. Kenny Baker, the small person inside what looks like an oversized Birdseye wrapper, found that taking one step inside Artoo thoroughly exhausted him.

As might be expected, a sequel is in the works for *Star Wars,* but who will win Leia's affection is still a mystery.

(Top) The life-size version of the Falcon took up the space of an entire sound stage when finished.

(Center) Here, one of the miniature versions of the Falcon is supposedly suspended in mid-air. What's the trick? It's being propped up on the other side.
(Bottom) Dykstra checks out lighting involving the Millenium Falcon. A blue screen will later have effects projected on it. This is one of the three sizes built of the ship. There is one smaller version and one life-size that's seen docked in the Death Star.

# The Man Behind the Magic

It's been said more than once that for an actor, the stage is the preferred medium. For the producer, it's television, and for the director, it's movies that hold all the honors. Recently, however, writers, editors and special effects men have also come into the limelight and deservedly so. Their contribution to the film industry has more or less gone unnoticed up until a few years ago.

John Dykstra is one of these people. In 1975, George Lucas called Dykstra to tell him about the new film he was planning, named *Star Wars.* Lucas well remembered Dykstra's work under Douglas Trumbull on such films as the *Andromeda Strain,* not to mention the highly underrated *Silent Running.*

What Lucas wanted, according to Dykstra, were special effects that involved spacecrafts engaged in acrobatic stunts "Wrong Way" Corrigan would have been proud of. Under Trumbull's tutelage, Dykstra set about the task which would take some two years to accomplish.

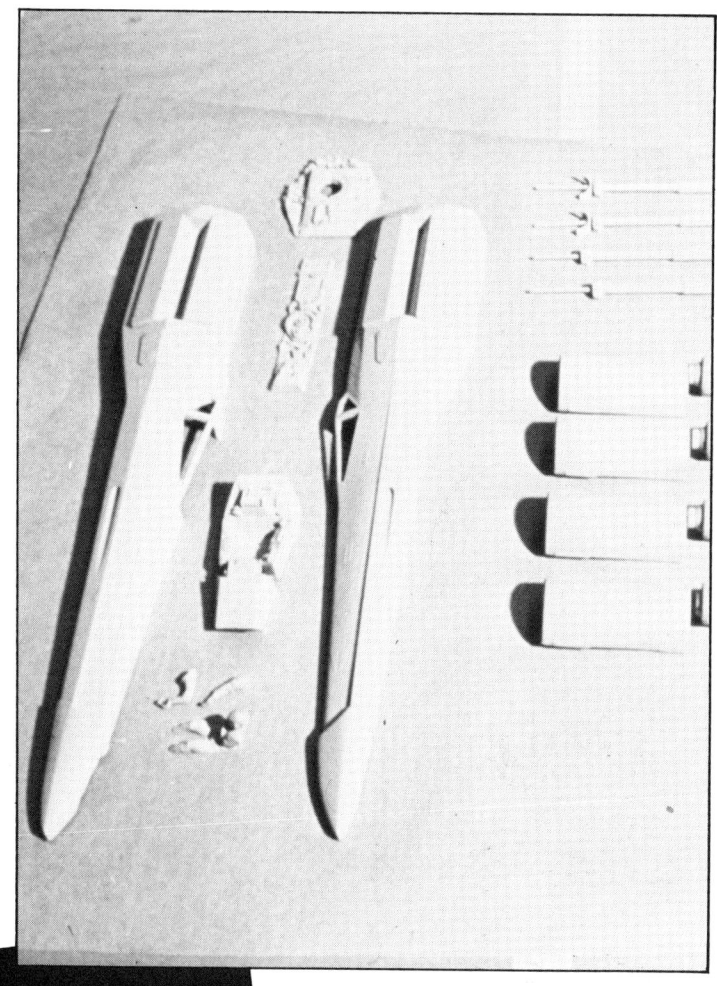

(Top) Most miniatures were constructed from parts of already existing model plane kits.
(Left) A completed miniature of the Galactic Cruiser with explosive mechanisms built in its engines.

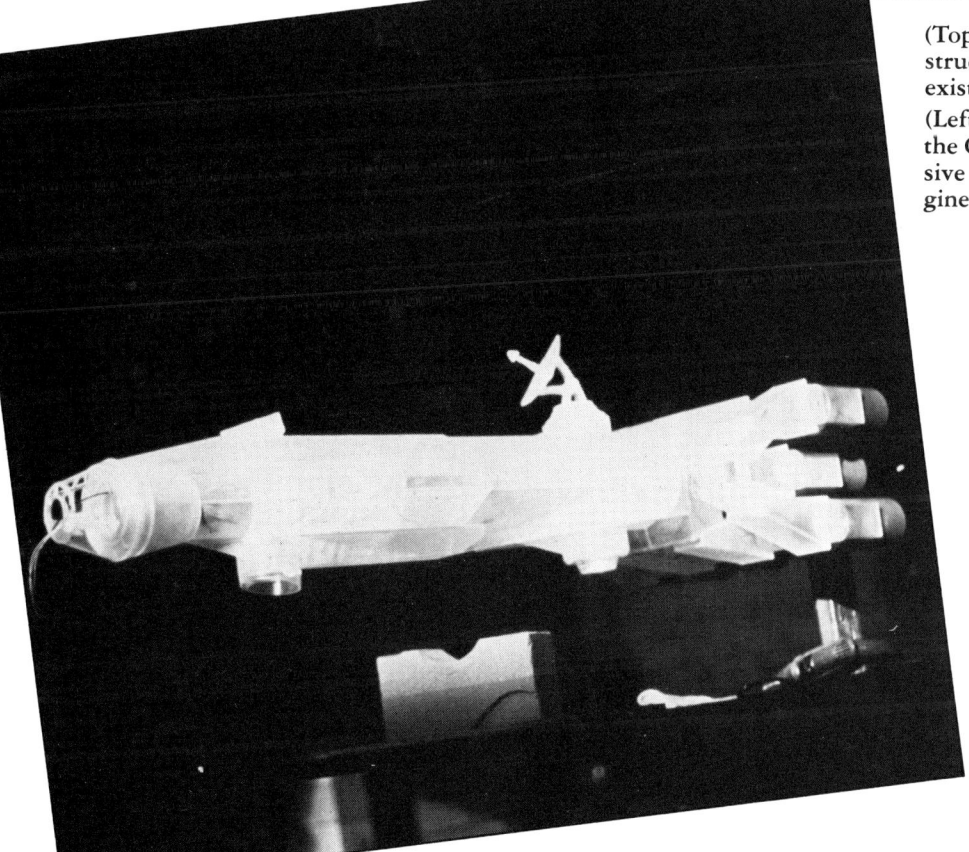

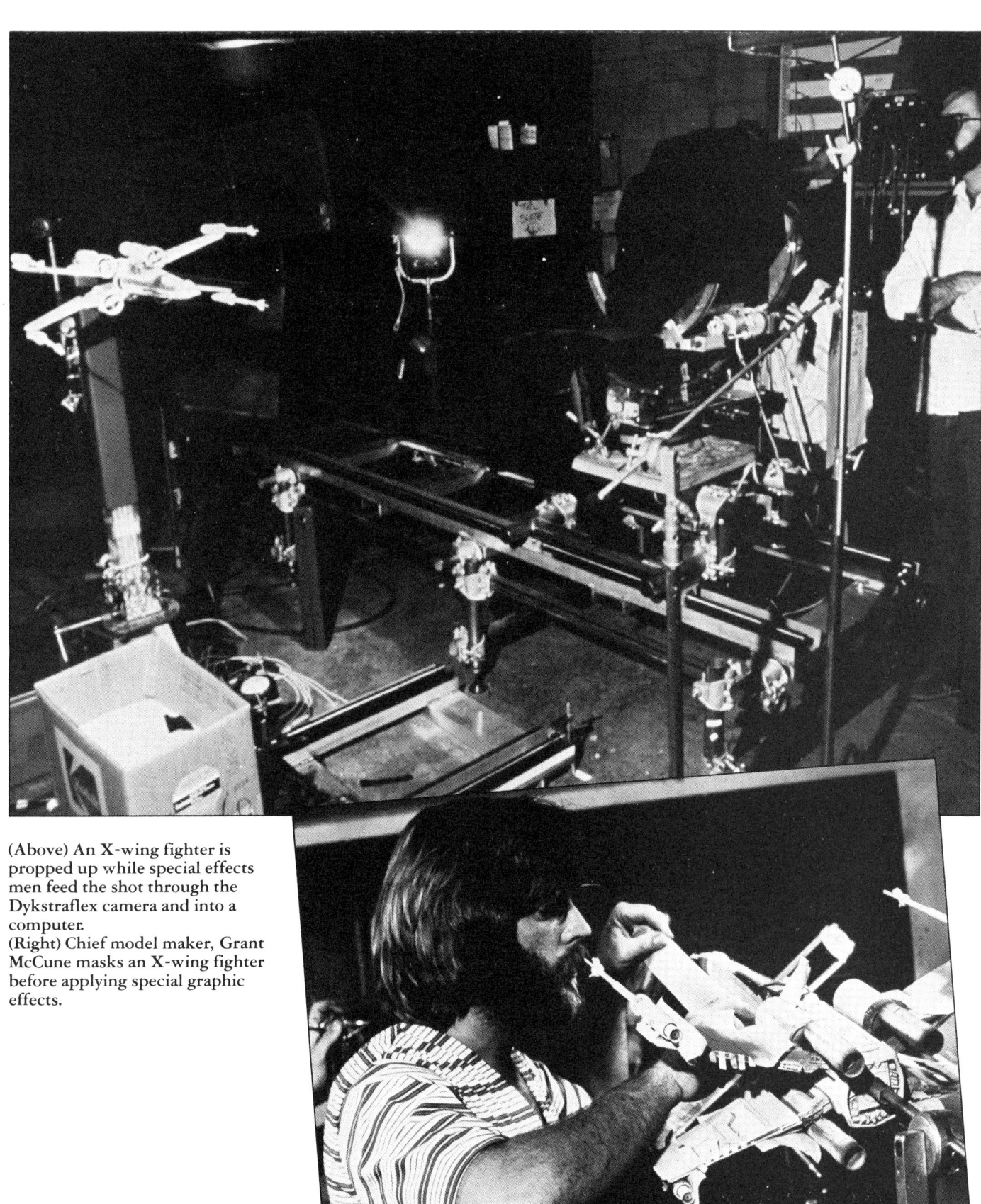

(Above) An X-wing fighter is propped up while special effects men feed the shot through the Dykstraflex camera and into a computer.
(Right) Chief model maker, Grant McCune masks an X-wing fighter before applying special graphic effects.

All in all, there are over 365 special effects in *Star Wars*. Miniature effects, photographic effects, you name it! Housing a production as mammoth as *Star Wars* at first proved a problem, until an old warehouse was purchased and converted into a special effects studio aptly tagged "Industrial Light and Magic, Inc."

When final count was taken, close to nine hundred technicians, model builders, special effects experts and jack-of-all trades were employed in the course of both pre and post production.

In many cases, *Star Wars'* special effects were often simpler than they looked. Luke's landspeeder, for example, appeared to fly a foot or two off the ground. In reality, this was achieved by simply lining the bottom of the vehicle with mirrors, which reflected the Tunisian sands perfectly, giving the image of weightlessness.

Perhaps the most stunning effect in *Star Wars* was the Millennium Falcon's jump into hyperspace. The effect was so dazzling that audiences all over unanimously break into cheers each time it's seen. The secret to hyperspace jump was only semi-complex, but required months of tedious camera work. The camera was used to film a backdrop of outerspace dotted with stars. The film was shot one frame at a time, moving the camera and the backdrop simultaneously after each shot.

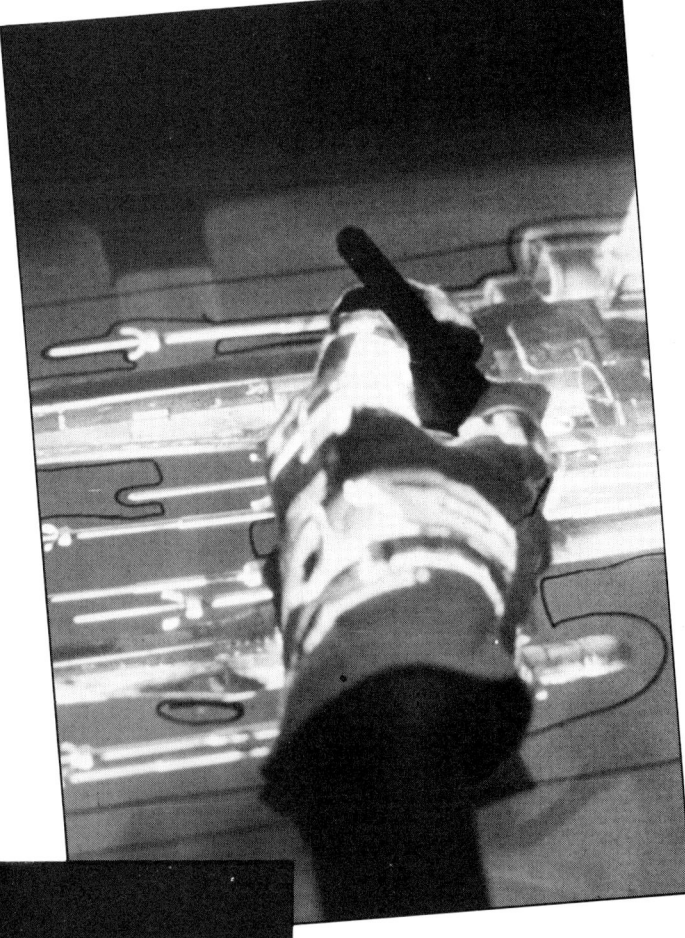

(Above) An artist outlines the X-wing fighters. Later this outline will then be opaqued to provide one section of a whole series that will be animated for a battle sequence.
(Left) A finished scene with two X-wing fighters maneuvering aerobatically against a star dotted background.

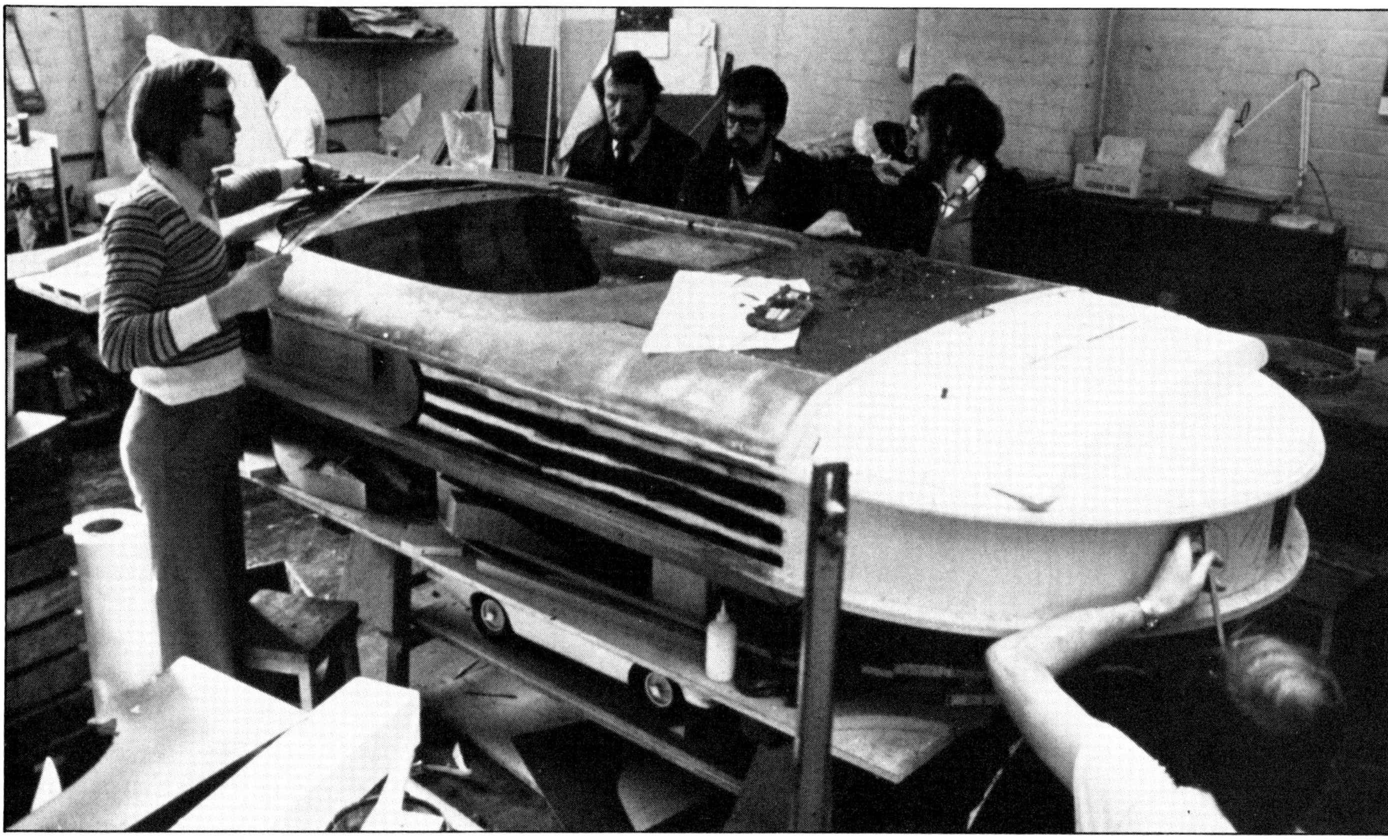

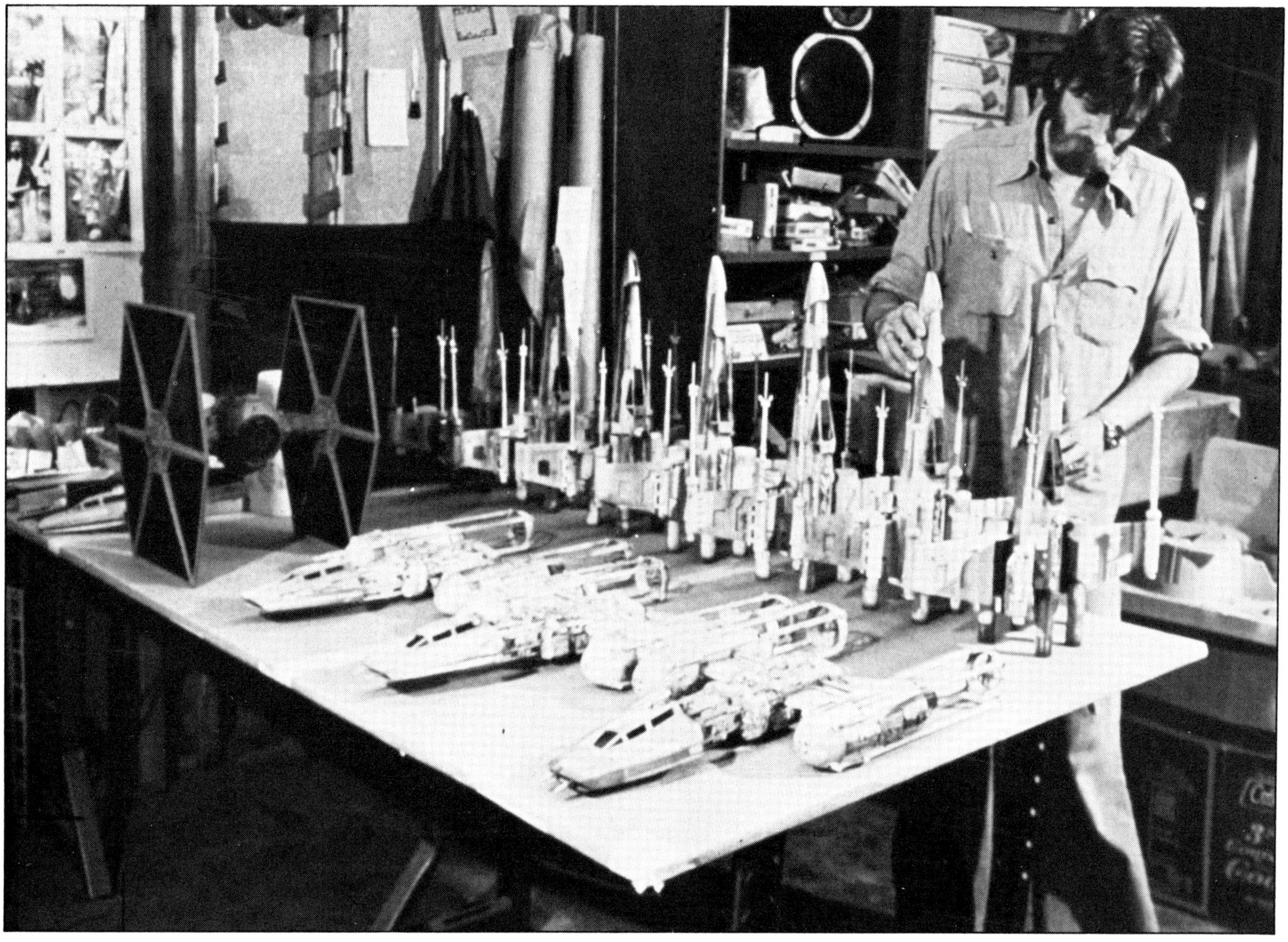

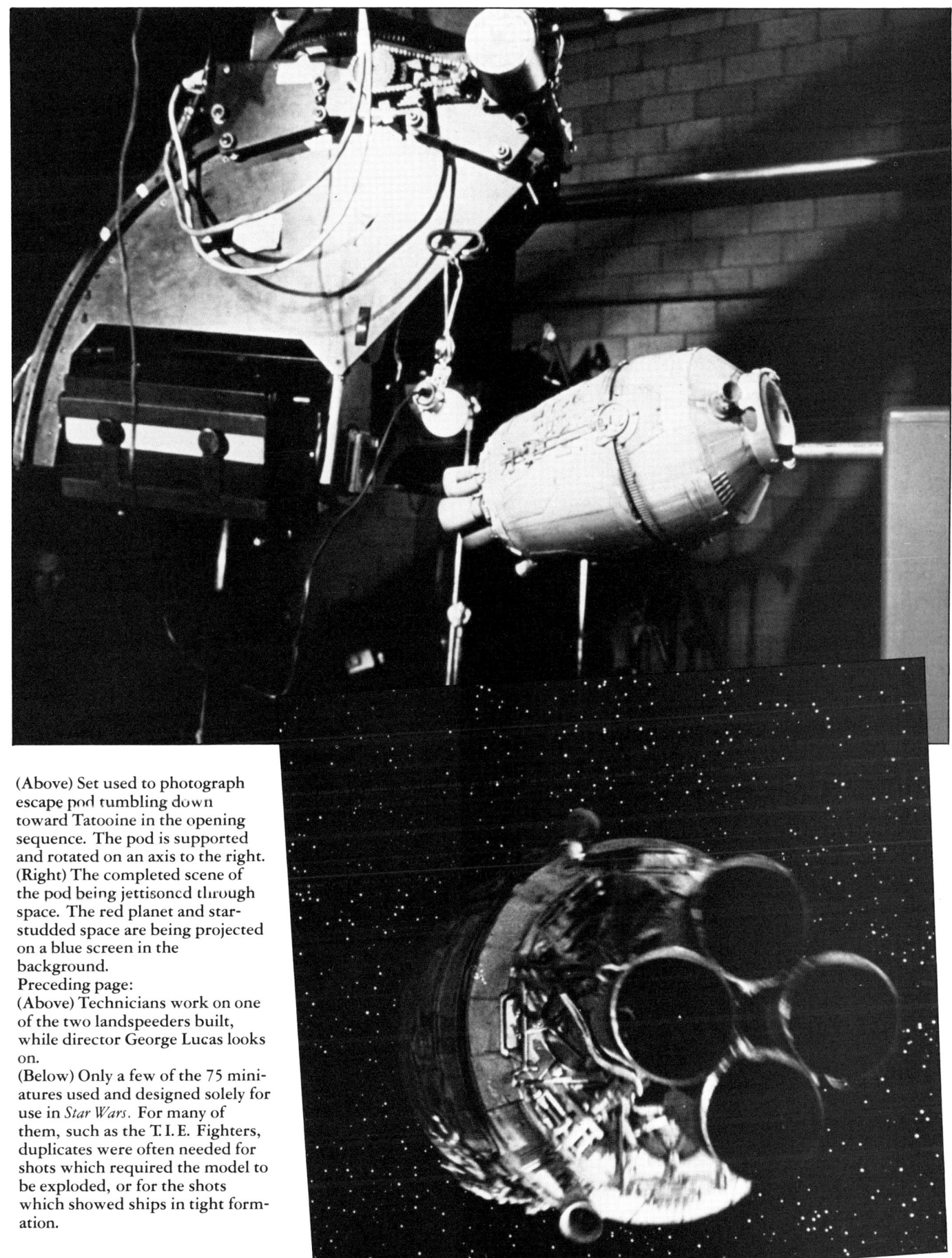

(Above) Set used to photograph escape pod tumbling down toward Tatooine in the opening sequence. The pod is supported and rotated on an axis to the right.
(Right) The completed scene of the pod being jettisoned through space. The red planet and star-studded space are being projected on a blue screen in the background.
Preceding page:
(Above) Technicians work on one of the two landspeeders built, while director George Lucas looks on.
(Below) Only a few of the 75 miniatures used and designed solely for use in *Star Wars*. For many of them, such as the T.I.E. Fighters, duplicates were often needed for shots which required the model to be exploded, or for the shots which showed ships in tight formation.

(Top) The foam parts from which the Death Star surface was constructed were nearly indestructible. The section seen here in the middle had weathered seven major explosions with little deterioration. For filming of the explosions, the operation was moved outdoors because this provided the perfect source of light needed for such photography. (Below) Sixteen hundred square feet of the Death Star surface were built for the famous finale. In order to create the effect of being in the pilot's seat, the Dykstraflex was suspended in the "trench" and reeled across.

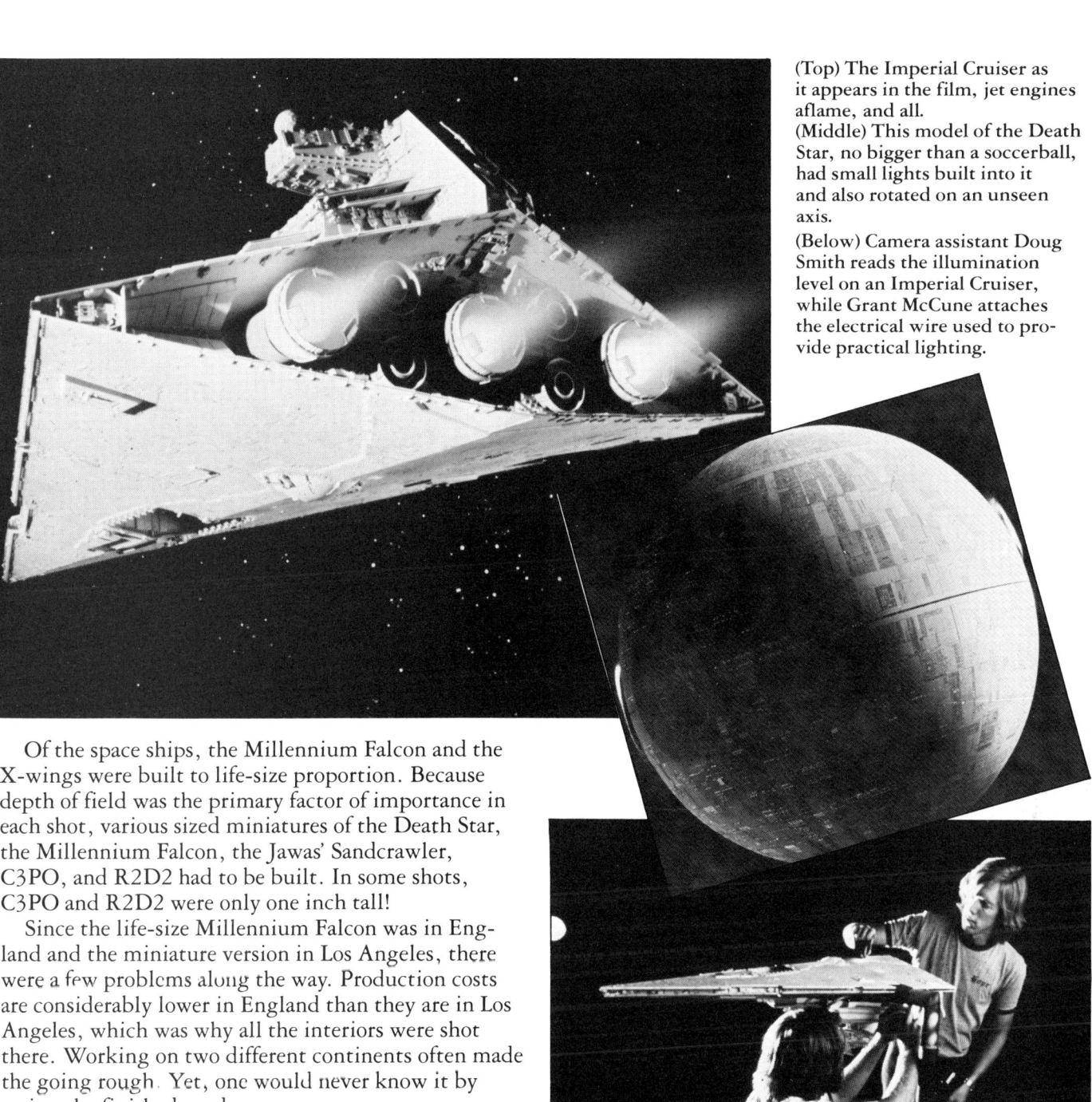

(Top) The Imperial Cruiser as it appears in the film, jet engines aflame, and all.
(Middle) This model of the Death Star, no bigger than a soccerball, had small lights built into it and also rotated on an unseen axis.
(Below) Camera assistant Doug Smith reads the illumination level on an Imperial Cruiser, while Grant McCune attaches the electrical wire used to provide practical lighting.

Of the space ships, the Millennium Falcon and the X-wings were built to life-size proportion. Because depth of field was the primary factor of importance in each shot, various sized miniatures of the Death Star, the Millennium Falcon, the Jawas' Sandcrawler, C3PO, and R2D2 had to be built. In some shots, C3PO and R2D2 were only one inch tall!

Since the life-size Millennium Falcon was in England and the miniature version in Los Angeles, there were a few problems along the way. Production costs are considerably lower in England than they are in Los Angeles, which was why all the interiors were shot there. Working on two different continents often made the going rough. Yet, one would never know it by seeing the finished product.

The biggest contribution of John Dykstra and his crew, not only to *Star Wars,* but to the entire film industry, is the Dykstraflex. This special camera was invented in order to accomplish the 365 composite opticals. The camera was linked to a sophisticated computer which recorded and memorized every shot.

(Left) John Williams doing what he does best—making music.

# Notes On Composer John Williams

In the spring of 1975, director Steven (*Jaws*) Spielberg first introduced George Lucas to composer John Williams. In December of 1975, Lucas gave Williams the *Star Wars* script to read.

"Normally," said 45 year-old, New York-born Williams, "I try not to read scripts because you tend to form your own images of the characters and locales in your mind."

George Lucas was a great help to Williams because he knew the idiom of music he wanted in the picture. Music was a special problem because the movie was so original and had so many unusual effects.

In Lucas' mind, electronic or concrete music would have been too obvious a choice. He wanted a stark contrast to his visuals. So he chose an almost 19th century romantic score against these yet unseen sights.

According to Williams, who spent a year preparing his ideas for the score, Lucas' instincts were correct. He felt that "the disparity of styles was right for this film."

While the approach may have been unusual for a futuristic film, composer John Williams felt it was appropriate. "The music relates to the characters and to the human problems; even for non-humans. I think this film is wildly romantic and fanciful. George and I both felt that the music should be full of high adventure and the soaring spirits of the characters in the film."

During March of 1977, Williams conducted the eighty-seven piece London Symphony Orchestra in a series of fourteen sessions in order to record the ninety minutes of original music for *Star Wars*.

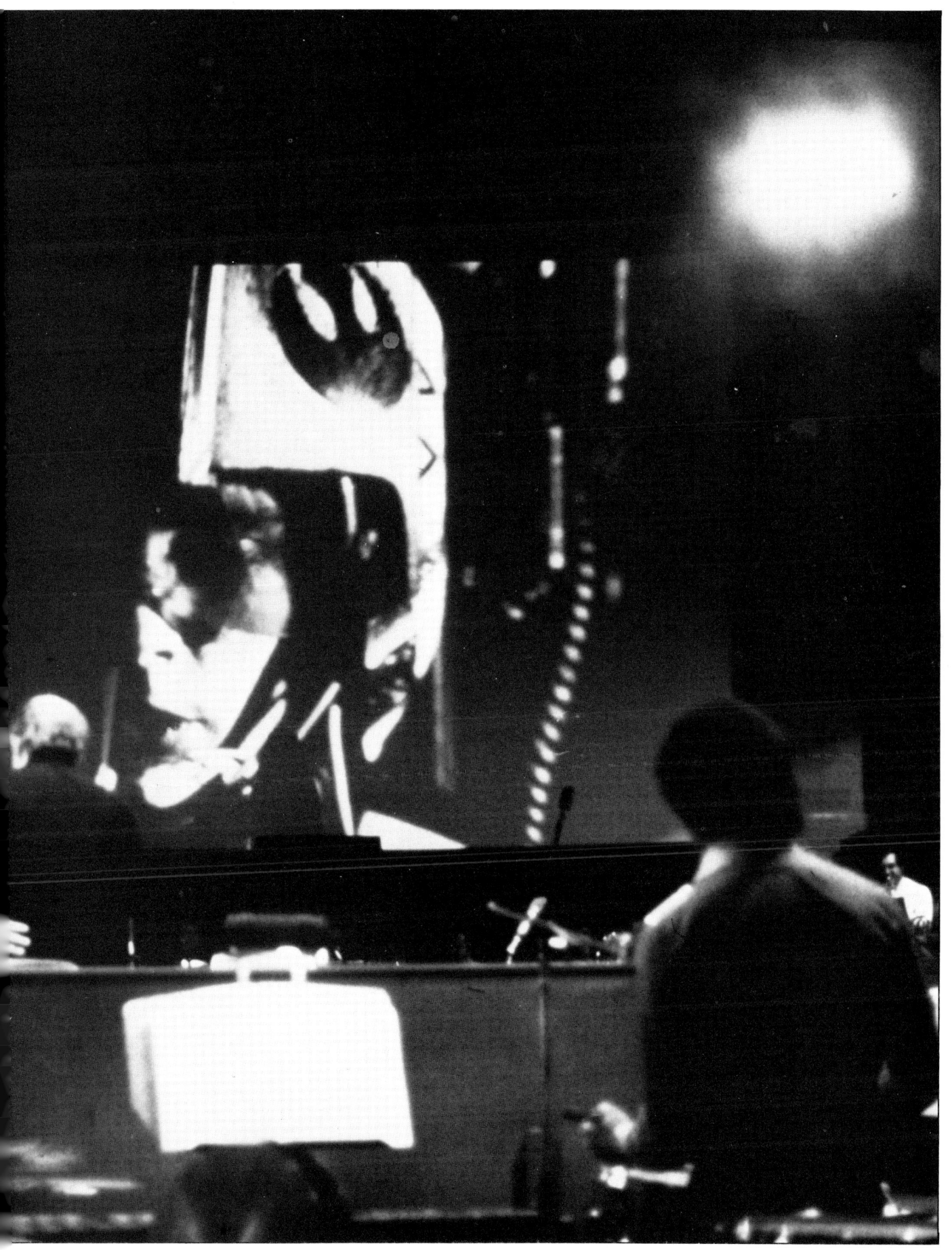

John Williams conducting the London Symphony Orchestra. Clips from the film are projected behind him.

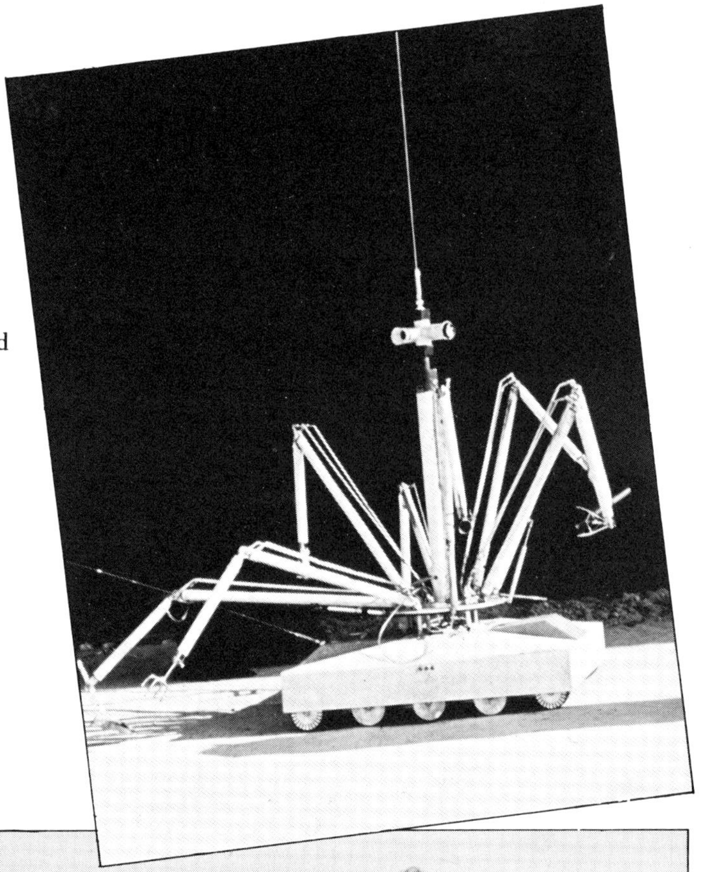

(Above right) This six armed droid could no doubt be used in many households as a live-in domestic.

(Center) One of the low-life droids, hanging around the cantina in Mos Eisley—no doubt looking for a one way passage out of town.
(Right) See Threepio, programmed for protocol, and the rambunctious Artoo Detoo, whose abilities were limitless. These two droids were definitely the show stoppers and real heroes of *Star Wars*.

# The Magnetic Metalmen

Lucas, as far as *Star Wars* is concerned, did his homework. Together with artist Ralph McQuarrie and special effects man, John Stears, Lucas instructed exactly what he wanted. Stears and his staff then talked with various experts in the field of robotics. Before they were through Stears and his crew talked with experts from St. Mary's College, London University and even artificial limb specialists at Queen Mary's Hospital, in Roehampton, London. With special help from the latter, Stears learned useful information regarding pneumatics and electronics, which gave the creators of *Star Wars* a new application to the field of robotics.

Since production costs for *Star Wars* were roughly $100,000 a day, fortunes were spent when the robot sequences ran into trouble. The scene with the Jawas, for instance, cost thousands. What with ten or twelve robots in that particular scene, with so many intricate parts, breakdowns were frequent.

With the first *Star Wars* in the can and grossing millions, Artoo Detoo and See Threepio will repeat their original roles in the sequel. This time around though they may give Bing Crosby and Bob Hope a run for their money with "The Road to Tatooine."

(Top) An artoo unit the Jawas had on display for Luke and his uncle. A taller and much older model than the others.
(Center) The mind probe, a dastardly robot who shot Princess Leia with truth serum.
(Bottom left) Two anonymous droids in the Jawas' Sandcrawler. The one on the right bears a striking resemblance to a gas pump with legs.

# Have Crew Will Travel

In 1936, Metro-Goldwyn-Mayer released *San Francisco* with Clark Gable and Spencer Tracy. The film culminated in the infamous San Francisco earthquake of 1906, and the special effects went unequalled for years. Until the 1950's anyway, when the one magic ingredient that made movie-going so enjoyable seemed to vanish—mainly, care and a lot of love.

George Lucas saw his role as a director to attempt to restore some of the love and affection that seemed lacking from current films. If this meant packing up and leaving for Tunisia, so be it, which in fact he did, along with a film production crew and several actors.

Needless to say, the making of *Star Wars* proved to be as much an epic as the film itself. In March of 1976, one hundred and thirty cast and crew members arrived in a sleepy little town called Tozeur, well within the depths of Tunisia. Eight grueling weeks of truly rigorous work produced the fictional planet of Tatooine. Whether Tozeur will become the new Hollywood is anyone's guess. *Star Wars* did prove to be a first rate travelog for Matmata, another town in Tunisia, where the inhabitants make their homes by carving them from the sides of crater-like holes.

Tunisia however, was not Tatooine's only home base. Other locations included Death Valley in Nevada, the setting for countless movie westerns, and the Tikal National Park in Guatamala was used for the shots of Yavin's lush vegetation.

Shooting in Tunisia proved to be more of a problem than director Lucas and his crew bargained for: there were more than just sandstorms to contend with; specially made goggles were supplied to shield everyone from the strapping winds; and Anthony Daniels, who played Threepio, found that the inside of his costume became unbearably hot after just several minutes, forcing him to come out for air every now and then. Cameramen were complaining that the sand was clogging up their cameras, which, as a result, had to be cleaned out each evening.

In the town of Matmata, where additional scenes were filmed, the interiors of Luke's home, for example, were shot in The Hotel Sidi Driss. Since Matmata is inhabited primarily by Troglodytes, it proved to be perfect for the filming of the futuristic and alternately primitive moisture farm. To protect themselves from the blistering heat and cold of Tunisia, the citizens of Matmata built their homes the way they did to good advantage.

(Above) Luke and Leia about to make their famous Death Star swing, actually thirty feet above ground.
(Left) Mirrors, lights and special painted glass gave the shaft its bottomless appearance.

(Right) The terrain in Tunisia was so rough that all equipment had to be transported by donkeys.
(Center) Two crewmen set up the "moisture farm" for a scene between Luke and his aunt.
(Below) To save time, two to three cameras would be used to cover several angles of a scene.

(Above) Carrie said, "It was difficult for me to hate Cushing in the film, because in real life he's such a sweetheart."
(Middle) The crew shaping Luke's destiny.
(Left) Cast and crew preparing for battle.

# Behind the Scenes

The making of *Star Wars* was as much an epic behind the cameras as it was in front. For over four months, one hundred and thirty cast and crew members trekked from one side of this planet to the other to seek the proper ingredients that make *Star Wars* the unique phenomenon it is.

In March of 1976, the film production crew landed in Tozeur. The crew worked rigorously for eight weeks — and finally Tozeur was transformed into Tatooine. Afterwards, cast and crew moved on to Matmata. The other location used as Tatooine was Death Valley in Nevada, and the Tikal National Park in Guatemala was used in the Yavin Jungle sequence.

The narrative began after the exterior shots were completed. Lucas and company moved to Elstree Studios outside London, as well as Shepperton Studio in Middlesex.

Each cast member had their own recollection of what life was like aboard "the gigantic playground" as actor Mark Hamill called it.

"Playing the role of Princess Leia was a lot of fun most of the time — but it sure wasn't fun all the time," says twenty-one year old Carrie Fisher. "After about two hours in the garbage room it started to wear off, my skin started to wrinkle and my rubber suit didn't fit any more!"

Harrison Ford as the mercenary, macho Han Solo had a more personal gripe. He was so dismayed by the banality of some of his dialogue ("I've been from one end of this galaxy to the other, kid...") that he threatened to tie up director George Lucas and force him to repeat his own lines!

For Mark Hamill life as Luke Skywalker was a time of sheer excitement, only occasionally mixed with tinges of tedium. In fact, when Hamill first got wind of the *Star Wars* project, he recalls, "I thought if they were making a big space fantasy movie, I'd be satisfied just to watch part of it being shot. I even asked my agent if she could get me onto the set so I could see how some of the special effects were being done." Instead, his agent got him the lead role in the film.

"The character of Luke," as Hamill explains, "is like Dorothy in *The Wizard of Oz*. They both are characters people look at to see how they react to things. They are simple, naive characters. All they want is a little adventure."

(Top) The Tusken Raiders' attack wasn't as scary as it looked.
(Bottom) Ben Kenobi and group rehearsing for their entry into Mos Eisley.

(Right) Unwitting extras who appeared as stormtroopers in *Star Wars* didn't know what they were getting themselves into as the temperature inside the stormtrooper uniforms grew unbearably hot.

(Below) The rigors of being Chewy included a two-hour make-up job for Peter Mayhew.

(Above) With *Star Wars* a hit, the future of Harrison Ford (Han Solo) seems well assured.

Hamill and Fisher each got their share of excitement when it came time for them to do their now famous *Tarzan and Jane* swing across the inside of the Death Star. "It would've been fun if they'd let us do it a second time," Fisher reminisces. "But it was like going on the upside down rollercoaster—we did it one time and that was scary—and then if we could've done it again, it might have been fun. I guess they didn't want to press their luck—considering we were thirty feet off the ground."

Alec Guinness talks about Ben, "The role was a combination of wizards and sorcerers. We took a little from here and there, but it all worked well."

David Prowse (Lord Darth Vader) and Peter Mayhew (Chewbacca) have only dabbled in acting. Prowse is a retired undefeated heavyweight champion. Mayhew worked as a porter in a London hospital. Both were cast for their height and presence.

Anthony Daniels (See Threepio) made his film debut a few years ago, working mostly on London stage and television. The 3-foot-8-inch Kenny Baker (Artoo Detoo) spent almost thirty years in show business. He formed an act called the Mini Tones, touring Europe and North Africa.

Peter Cushing (Grand Moff Tarkin) is one of the great perpetuators of screen villainy. Since most of the script is based on Flash Gordon-type characters, Cushing fit right in as the dastardly Ming's counterpart.

Now having "swashbuckled" their way through the first *Star Wars,* Mark Hamill, Carrie Fisher, and Harrison Ford have become real veteran space cadets. When production for the sequel begins, it's going to take a lot more than dark Lord Darth Vader to scare this defiant trio!

(Right) David Prowse and fencing partner (left) rehearse the movements for the famous duel with mock swords. The swords in the film were coated to give them the laser effect.

(Left) The gauntness in Peter Cushing's face gives him that added coldness for the character of the Grand Moff Tarkin. During a break in the filming a make-up woman does a quick retouch job on Cushing.

(Right) David Prowse as the dastardly Darth Vader struts down a corridor on the set of the Death Star. Cinematographer Gilbert Taylor has the camera propped at a low angle in order to make Darth look more immense.

(Left) Anthony Daniels being straw fed by a crewman Daniels sweated off close to four pounds a day.
(Below) Kenny Baker in-between takes.

(Left) Each day Anthony Daniels was helped into his C3PO costume. During film breaks, since it was impossible for him to sit down, the crew propped him up.

(Right) Alec Guinness and Mark Hamill rehearse the scene where Obi-Wan Kenobi brings Luke back to consciousness.
(Below) Hamill, Guinness, producer Kurtz and director Lucas toast Sir Alec on his 62nd birthday.

(Right) Two technicians give an R-2 model the once over.
(Left) For long shots of the Jawas' Sandcrawler a miniature was used. In the background the life-size bottom half of the Sandcrawler is seen.

## Star Wars Sequels

Will there be a sequel to *Star Wars?* Absolutely! Already there is a full-length feature film scheduled, due in fall of 1978.

Lucas has indicated that he will only serve as executive producer. Still, a whole slew of questions are left up in the air: Will his hero marry the strong willed, but willing Princess Leia? Or, will he have to challenge Han Solo to a duel for Leia's hand?

Mark Hamill, Carrie Fisher, and Harrison Ford will continue in their original roles; but what will become of Darth Vader? As for Artoo Detoo and See Threepio, *Star Wars* fans everywhere can be certain these loveable droids will be right back in the thick of things.

So until fall of 1978, when audiences return to that special time "long ago, in a galaxy far, far away," may The Force be with you.

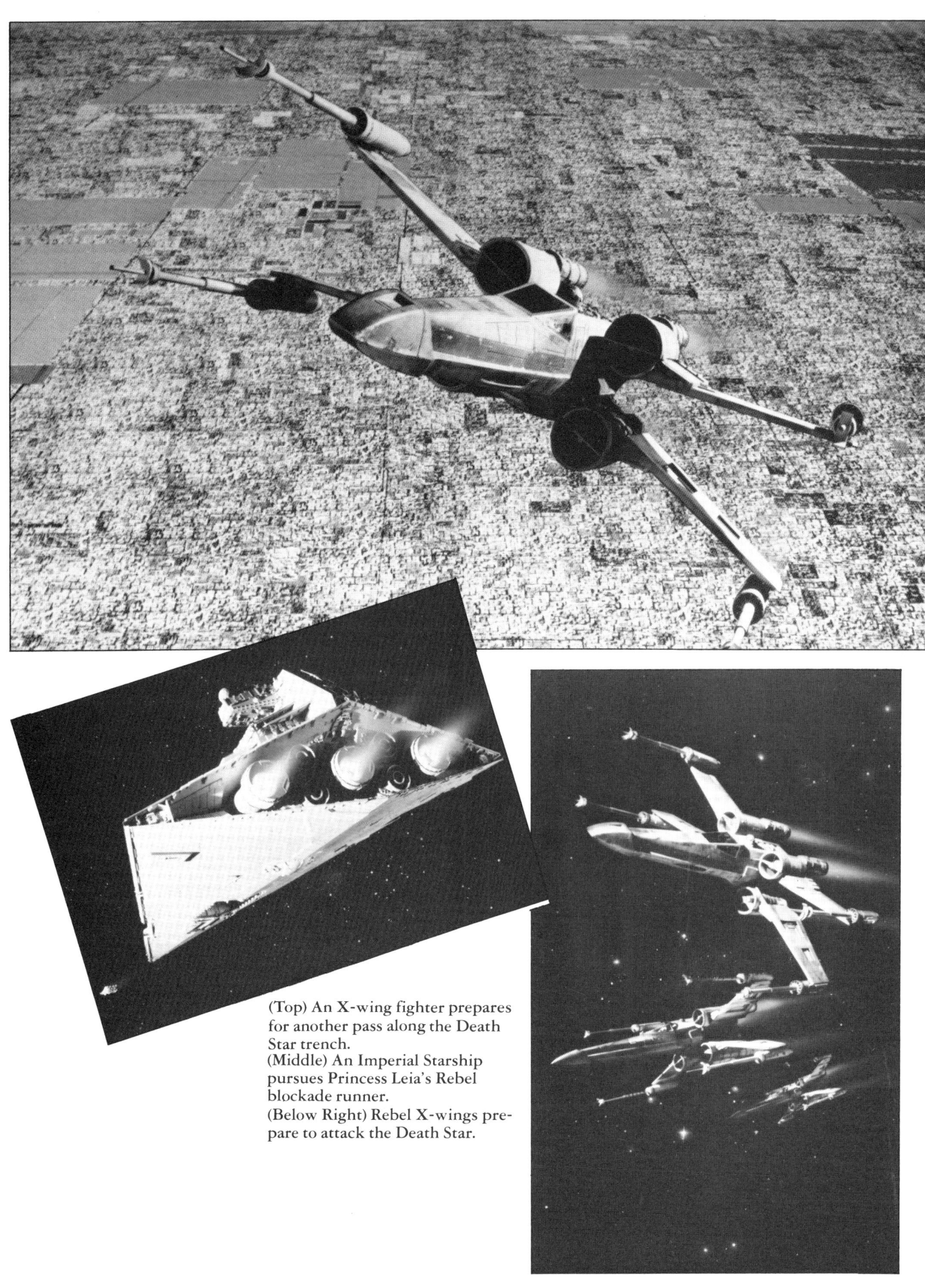

(Top) An X-wing fighter prepares for another pass along the Death Star trench.
(Middle) An Imperial Starship pursues Princess Leia's Rebel blockade runner.
(Below Right) Rebel X-wings prepare to attack the Death Star.

# Star Wars Glossary

**Alderaan** - *n.* peaceful planet, home of Princess Leia.

**Anchorhead** - *n.* small town on Tatooine, hangout for Luke and his chums.

**Android** - *n.* 1. having human shape 2. an automaton made to simulate a human being 3. a humanoid robot.

**Artoo Detoo** - *n.* R2D2, a stubby tripodal android who emits chirps, bleeps as a form of

communication, and projects holographic images.

**Banthas** - *n.* prehistoric type mammals used on moisture farms.

**Binders** - *n.* handcuffs.

**Bocce** - *n.* language spoken on Tatooine, needed to run a moisture farm.

**cantina** - *n.* a saloon in the center of Mos Eisley. Low-life and pilots hang out in it.

**Chewbacca** - *n.* a Wookiee, co-pilot and sidekick to Han Solo; sometimes called "The Walking Rug."

**Clone Wars** - *n.* most recent attempt by the Jedi Knights to stop the Imperial forces.

**Death Star** - *n.* space station the size of a planet, home base for the Imperial Forces with the firepower to destroy an entire planet.

**deflector shield** - *n.* a mask like implement that covers the face against laser beams.

**Dia-noga** - *n.* a snake-like creature which inhabits the garbage hatch.

**Droid** - *n.* shortened form of Android.

**Empire** - *n.* the governing body of the local star systems, a dictatorship.

**Force** - *n.* unseen energy field generated by all living things; it is similar to a universal religion to those who believe in its existence. Obi-Wan Kenobi and Luke have positive Force Lord Darth Vader has negative Force.

**hologram** - *n.* transmission beamed by an android which projects three-dimensional images.

**Imperial Cruisers** - *n.* immense spaceships used by the Imperial Empire to ferret out and destroy any opposition.

**Jawas** - *n.* rodent-like, three-feet-high creatures who travel the deserts of Tatooine. They collect and sell scrap metal, speak in low gutteral hisses, and have an unpleasant smell.

**Kenobi, Obi-Wan** - *n.* 1. a hermit who lives in the deserts of Tatooine. 2. one-time leader of the Jedi Knights, 3. a threat to the Imperial Empire due to his special mystical powers.

**Landspeeder** - *n.* another name for a landrover, a vehicle that is air propelled and needs no wheels.

**lubrication bath** - *n.* another name for an oil bath, used to clean the intricate insides of droids and robots.

**macrobinoculars** - *n.* super long-range telescope viewers.

**Millennium Falcon** - *n.* 1. space vehicle owned by Han Solo, freighter pilot and part-time smuggler. Faster than an Imperial craft,

the Falcon can jump into hyperspace.
**moisture farm** - *n.* its primary purpose is to supply water to the inhabitants of Tatooine.
**Mos Eisley** - *n.* a town on Tatooine that is the center of the spaceport low-life.
**Old Republic** - *n.* the governing body of the Alderaan star system that began to lose its grip when the Imperial Empire came into power.
**Organa, Leia,** - *n.* the senator from Alderaan. Young, headstrong and iron-willed, she uses her political position to gather information against the Imperial Empire.
**parsec** - *n.* a measurement of distance.
**restraining bolt** - *n.* a lug nut used to control the actions of an android or robot.
**Robot** - *n.* a mechanical man.
**Sandpeople** - *n.* marginally human creatures who inhabit the deserts of Tatooine; a vicious group of bandits, also known as Tusken Raiders.
**See Threepio** - *n.* C3P0, a humanoid robot. An android made of gold, he is programmed for protocol, feels emotions and worries a lot, can understand over a thousand intergalactic languages and can communicate with robots and other androids.
**Skywalker, Luke** - *n.* a twenty-year-old farm boy who lives on Tatooine, and yearns for excitement and adventure.
**Solo, Han** - *n.* cynical captain of the Millennium Falcon, and confident smuggler who hangs out in Mos Eisley.
**Stormtroopers** - *n.* drones used as armored soldiers by the Imperial Empire.
**Tarkin, Grand Moff** - *n.* governor of the Imperial Empire; the evil being who conceived and built the Death Star.
**Tatooine** - *n.* a neutral planet in the rebellion; home of Luke Skywalker; planet with twin suns.
**tractor beam** - *n.* an invisible anti-gravitational energy that is projected from the depths of the Death Star.
**Tusken Raiders** - *n.* see Sandpeople.
**T. I. E. fighters** - *n.* fierce little spaceships used by the Imperial Empire, which carry heavy fire power, and travel at an incredible rate.
**Vader, Darth** - *n.* one-time Jedi Knight and pupil of Obi-Wan Kenobi. Lured by the dark side of The Force, tall and malevolent, he assists Tarkin with his extrasensory powers toward the elimination of the Rebel Alliance.
**Wookiee** - *n.* eight-foot-high, fur-covered anthropoid with a quasi-monkey face and clear blue eyes, who can live for hundreds of years, and expresses only approval and disapproval through various kinds of grunts and growls.
**X-fighters** - *n.* spaceships used by the Rebel Alliance in their fight against the Imperial Empire. Agile and accurate, they are small enough to penetrate the Death Star.
**Y-fighters** - *n.* basically similar to X-fighters, with a slight change in formation.
**Yavin** - *n.* Lushly vegetated, uninhabited planet that houses the remaining Rebel base.

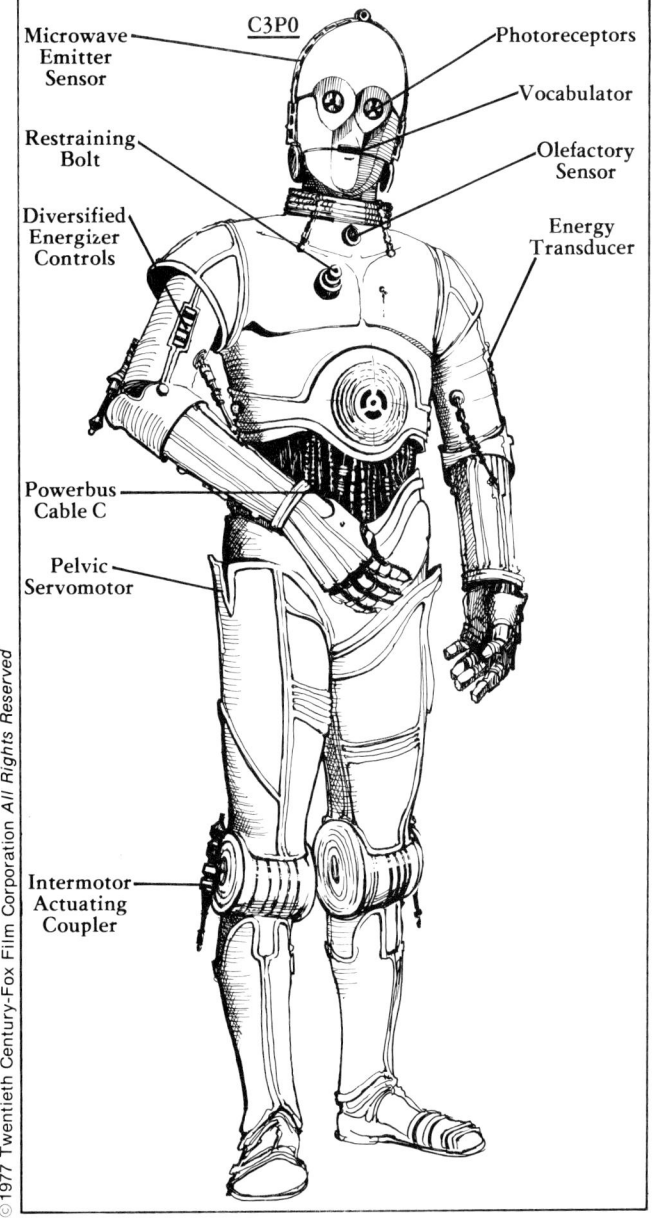